CLEAR WATER TROUT FISHING WITH WORM

By the same author

THE ART OF LAKE FISHING

PIKE ON THE PLUG

THE SPENCER LAKE FERTILITY CHART

SALMON AND SEATROUT IN WILD PLACES

NEWLY FROM THE SEA

WAYS OF FISHING

GAME FISHING TACTICS

Clear Water Trout Fishing With Worm

By

SIDNEY SPENCER

H. F. & G. WITHERBY LTD

32 AYLESBURY STREET, LONDON, EC1R 0ET

Re-issued as a separate volume 1977
First published in 1935
and in 1972 reprinted with amendments
to form Part Two of the Author's
Ways of Fishing

Reprinted 1985

ISBN 0 85493 125 2

Printed in Great Britain by
Ebenezer Baylis and Son Limited
The Trinity Press, Worcester, and London

TO THE MEMORY OF MY FATHER, DONOR OF MY FIRST ROD AND COMPANION OF MY EARLY FISHING DAYS BY THE BURNS AND LITTLE HILL RIVERS

The Bridge Pool

Contents

Acknowledgement

Permission to include the two photographs on page 57 was kindly given by Mr. Hugh Falkus.

Prologue

I have had, and still have much to say about the study of our game fishes and their responses in varying conditions to the presentation of flies, lines and bait of all sorts and kinds. The subject is indeed limitless. But, for the most part, because my writings have concerned the imponderables in angling on which only recklessness will pontificate my advice has reflected opinion and suggestion - unassertive guidance rather than emphatic instruction.

A book on clear-water worming written in the thirties did however depart from this discipline for the plain reason that the average trout fisher then, as now, knew relatively little about the craft of taking trout in low clear water. The material of the original work was re-published in 1972 as Book II of *Ways of Fishing* and is again out of print. In this, its third appearance, the text is a version modernized in minor detail only.

Summer streams of the North and West are the places for this fishing and its practice where water is suitable is only limited by strictures which, in some areas and over-fished rivers, Water Authorities nowadays impose, a little sweepingly I think, on all bait fishing. Tackle and designations of tackle have changed since I first wrote on this subject but the basic art has not altered one whit since long before my time, nor in a hundred years.

Success in trout fishing, whatever the method, comes most readily from knowledge of the fish, their habits and ways, and of the places where they may be found. Clear water worm fishing is a branch of the art which teaches, *as no other can*, the ways of the trout. This follows from the fact that the worm-fisher seeks his fish in their lies, in conditions which expose to his observation the wide range of trout haunts and their occupants' behaviour. He works the water slowly and stealthily, studies to be quiet and concealed in his background and in the clear pools sees many things that are hidden from his rise-hunting and wider ranging friend with a fly rod.

Clear water worm fishing is a superb foundation on which to build or improve a knowledge of trout and trout fishing though it is far from being a simple technique for a beginner because it is, in certain respects decidedly *more difficult than fly work* – either wet or dry.

If, however, you are too cunning to sell a hen on a wet day, you have the makings of a clear-water worm fisher. If, in addition, you are knowledgeable about cover and background and the entire craft of staying hidden you can in time be a professor in this most exacting of all ways of fishing.

SIDNEY SPENCER

1

Upstream Worming in Perspective

CLEAR-WATER worm fishing must be placed in a class by itself. Fewer anglers really excel in it than in any other method. Even in the specialized and naturally attractive branches of game fish angling such as, for instance, nymph fishing and the localized methods like dapping or creeper-fishing, there are probably more accomplished enthusiasts than there are in the art of Stoddart and Stewart.

At first sight this may appear a little odd, in view of the undoubted and fairly widely recognized success of clear-water worm when it is properly handled; one might expect some popularity for the method. The fact of the matter is, however, that the average beginner without guidance from an experienced hand is apt to retire early from the game, first essays in worm fishing being, as a rule, inclined to produce nothing better than fingerling trout or parr. Care and study are really necessary to take good fish, and the fishing calls for a more precise technique than most anglers are in the habit of applying to, say, wet-fly, where persistence and a certain deftness in the rod-hand will bring *some* measure of success. I would never belittle proficiency with the fly rod – but I do consider that much less river-craft is necessary than in worm fishing. After all, the persistent fly fisher is able to cover a great deal more water than the bait fisherman and he may easily get results if he can throw a good line. Even if he does not understand where precisely to expect his fish he will get far more than a bait fisher of similar inexperience. In worm fishing in clear water mere manipulative ability will never result in bags of trout. Style hardly counts. Skill in this fishing has a wider implication than in most others, and from the very nature of the method there must be difficulties unknown in either wet or dry fly.

It makes infinitely greater demands upon your knowledge of the river and the trout than fly work or spinning, both of which are more or less long range methods. Practised at the proper season, when streams are low and crystal clear and brilliant sunlight pours down on pool and stickle, showing up every pebble on the bottom, worm fishing is delicate work for the expert and tantalizingly difficult fishing for anyone else. I believe that there still persists in some quarters an idea that all worm fishing is a dirty business from more than one point of view. The more serious implication is, of course, that it is an easy way of murdering trout, and therefore unsportsmanlike. Nothing could be farther from the truth.

I have never met anyone holding these views who had the sincerity to put his beliefs to the test, though I have on more than one occasion offered to supply the disapproving one with an outfit, accompany him to the river and there instruct him in the rudiments of worm fishing. I am perfectly confident that each and every one of these men would have returned from the waterside very much disillusioned, and, let us hope, enlightened.

Sheer misunderstanding is at the root of the trouble in most cases and clear-water fishing is confused with and shares in the odium attaching to spate fishing, which is a vastly different thing. And, for that matter, though it does not really concern us here, even spate fishing is not quite a 'chuck and chance it' game – even the country boy fishing in a roaring brown flood does not catch trout without knowing where they are at such a time. But this kind of fishing is in no way comparable with clear-water work which, in its proper place, is a perfectly fair and sporting method of taking trout at times when fly may be all but hopeless in the daytime.

It covers, firstly, all the knowledge of trout ways and habits that comes from unceasing close observation, plus an acute river-sense – an instinctive appreciation of conditions and trout reaction to them. Secondly, it includes the ability to appraise a pool, a run, or a section of the stream, and to decide where the trout are likely to be and how and where they can best be approached. Lastly, there is ordinary handiness in managing rod and tackle, but this kind of skill is easiest to acquire, and much less costly in time.

Certain essentials in worm fishing govern all procedure. Suitable conditions are always such that to fish 'fine and far off' might seem to offer the only chance of success. Fineness *is* necessary and is simply attained, but 'far off' tactics, in the accepted sense of the term, are impossible, and herein are complications. It is absolutely essential, and an inflexible rule of the game that *one must be in constant direct contact with the bait,* as otherwise in nine cases out of ten, bites go undetected. The bait must be under control from the moment when it enters the water, and the line recovery smooth and unflurried.

Because of this, and of the fact that the bait is placed ahead of the angler, generally in fast water, it is not possible to fish 'far off'. Here is a set of circumstances found in no other fishing. The angler must fish with a short line (to keep contact with his bait) in crystal clear water, often under a brilliant sun, yet remain unseen by his quarry. Here it is that the cunning of the river-wise plays its part and, with the right rod, goes some way towards reducing the odds against the angler.

2

Rod and Tackle

A ROD for upstream worm fishing must have certain rather special qualities; it differs from a fly rod to as great an extent, and in much the same way, as a rod suited to tight-line fishing for roach. Before describing it I should perhaps tell you why its distinctive features are necessary. In other branches of angling there is room for experiment with rod lengths, types of construction, and actions, and the best, in most cases, is that with which the user does best and in which he has most confidence. In worm-fishing no such latitude exists, for the very nature of the fishing keeps you within very narrow limits in your selection of a rod. Personal preferences can concern only the minor details, and though you may vary these according to fancy, you must preserve in the rod certain distinctive features.

First then, the rod must be long, as trout rods go. When you picture in your mind's eye the all too numerous tribulations of a hot summer's day on the well-bushed banks of the average small stream, you may think a long rod, and the weight that it seems to imply, something of a burden. That is a commonsense view, of course, but you must resist the temptation to use a short rod with the idea of travelling light in deference to the weather conditions. Besides, the rod for this work is by no means as heavy as a fly rod of similar length, so you need not judge it by that standard.

Remember that your line must always be short and that your chances of detection by the fish are increased accordingly. If, in addition, you use a short rod, you increase your handicap enormously. The ideal combination is a long rod, used with a relatively short line which will enable you to keep constant contact with the bait. There is another reason for length in the rod. You do not, in worm-fishing, employ a true cast to get your line out, and for this and other reasons the short rod is useless to reach distant runs and places which, if you were using fly, you could cover by getting out a long line. You have to work up to your fish, covering only modest distances ahead, and the long rod provides your only means of remaining at a discreet distance whilst still using the essential short line.

Taking everything into consideration, twelve feet is the most suitable length of a rod to be used on a variety of waters. Most of your fishing days will be spent on the smaller streams – those that might be classed as small rivers rather than as brooks – and though a big rod can be used on large open rivers like Tweed, Endrick, Lune and their larger tributaries, it would be a source of unending trouble, not to mention fatigue, on most days. Stoddart recommended a two-handed rod 'in length approaching to seventeen feet', while Stewart, in *The Practical Angler* says, 'The rod should not be shorter than from fourteen to sixteen feet.' Many changes have taken place since this advice was written, and the average length and weight of rods for every purpose has come down. There is reason to believe, too, that the average size of the trout has declined considerably.

It is doubtful whether a rod of over twelve to thirteen feet could be made light enough, without being floppy, to give any sport with the smallish trout that represent the average in most of our streams of today. But it *is* possible to make a *fairly* long rod light enough to fish single-handed, which can hardly have been possible with the limited range of materials available to rod-makers in Stoddart's time. So, whilst applauding the wisdom of his teaching, and that of Stewart, when they instruct in the use of long rods as opposed to short ones, we may confidently differ on the question of weight, and as to whether the rod is single- or double-handed in use.

I should add that experienced clear-water worm fishermen, even nowadays, do not lightly differ from Stewart and Stoddart; these men were masters of the game and much that they wrote is as sound today as when it was written.

But to return to the rod and its length. Quite apart from anything else, it is impossible to concentrate on fishing if you have to guide a long rod – a really long rod, I mean – through bushes and leafy tunnels. The best water is often the worst bushed, and it is annoying to have to pass over it, or to spoil it by floundering to and fro disentangling 'hang-ups'. The twelve feet rod suits the majority of rivers and streams from all points of view. It covers ample water ahead, is short enough to facilitate recovery of line even with trees overhead, and, if of the right type, is light enough to manipulate with one hand. This latter is most important.

In its action the rod must be stiff, not so stiff as to make it difficult to handle fish on very light tackle, but hard enough to swing outward and upward without showing a marked dipping motion of the top as the whole rod is urged forward. It should have no suspicion of top-heaviness because this fault grows in significance as you tire, and results in clumsy casting. This is bad, of course, in any rod, but the peculiar swinging 'cast' used in worming intensifies the evil. On the other hand, the rod must be firm in the top, not soft. It should transmit the firm lift of the strike at once and without preliminary wobbling, and the top should come to rest at once after a 'cast'.

For many years I found some of the good features in very light greenheart rods, but always there was something lacking. A serious objection was the brittleness of all except super-quality greenheart when worked down to small diameters.

Split cane, on the other hand I found to be too limber in a soft wet-fly actioned rod and too stiff when built for dry fly. Eventually I set out to design a rod which would incorporate the best points of the many I had tried.

The result was one of twelve feet in length and weighing eleven and a half ounces. The butt and centre piece are of whole cane and the top of split cane. It has an extra long cork grip, which, in conjunction with movable reel fittings, enables one to use the rod with one hand whatever one's length of arm, by resting the lower portion of the cork grip beneath the forearm. The reel fittings can be so placed that the reel hangs just below the wrist. The rod is finished in a dull and non-flashing enamel, and in colour an unobtrusive olive green.

This rod combines all those features which, in my experience, go to make up the ideal. Its action is better than that of any other worming rod that I have tried, though its specification approximates to those of occasional specimens on the market. Some of these are very good and you cannot go far wrong with a rod by a first-class maker. But wherever you buy your rod, be very sure that you get one with the proper action. Have it fitted with reel and line and draw off about eleven feet of line. On the end of this pinch four or five medium-sized shot. Now get the line swinging from the nearly upright rod in a wide arc. Let it swing towards and just past your elbow, then as it reaches almost the limit of its swing in the opposite direction urge the whole rod smartly upward and forward. Lower the rod so that the shot strikes the floor at the full stretch of the line and watch how quickly or how slowly the rod tip comes to rest. There should be no wobble or pronounced dip. This is the measure of just how stiff in the top a good worming rod should be.

If you remember, when you try a rod, that you do not cast overhead in worm-fishing, as you do in fly fishing, but swing the bait into position in the manner outlined above, I think you will recognize the right kind of action when you grasp the right rod. A small point worth watching is this. You do not change your grasp as often as when using a fly rod, and it is a great aid to comfort to have the bait-fishing rod fitted with a rather more rotund cork grip than is usual.

Almost any fly reel will do quite well, though I prefer a reel a shade heavier than is properly and theoretically suited to the rod. This is easier on the wrist throughout a long day and helps somewhat in guarding against tired dropping of the rod point. The modern narrow drum type reel is excellent because it is compact and less likely to catch on clothing than the older and wider types. Its quickness in line recovery is a useful quality, but one which is not in great demand in worm fishing. Most trout are hooked at close quarters, and, unless they are good ones, are played there.

A medium gauge fly line, all the better if it is tapered, will do splendidly. I strongly advise you to avoid the undressed and soft silk lines often suggested in tackle catalogues as being suitable for worm fishing. They have three very bad faults. In the first place they are very light and uncontrollable in a wind. They are inclined also to cling to the rod in wet weather – and you may often have low water conditions whilst it is raining, and lastly, deteriorate in the absence of constant attention much sooner than dressed lines. Normally you use very little of the line, except when you have to yield line in playing a good fish, and the bulk remains undisturbed on the reel. There it receives an occasional wetting and is exposed, more often, to strong sunlight, and speedily perishes. But because it is unused you are apt to take its strength for granted, and are equally apt to be disillusioned.

The only conceivable advantage in using an undressed line is, as far as I can see, that it might be more easily made to float than the dressed line, but this is a weak argument in its favour because, strictly speaking, the line should not be in the water at all. If you use a very long line – long for worm-fishing, that is – and a short cast, you might possibly have a little line in the water at times, but not otherwise. As a rule not more than five or six feet of line will be out beyond the rod tip, and only the last three feet or so of the nylon cast will be in the water. The less running tackle you have below the surface the better.

As regards the length that should be on the reel, you will find twenty-five yards ample whilst fishing the average trout stream, but if you are likely to fish often in rivers where you may encounter sea-trout or even an odd salmon, you should have forty or fifty yards of line and backing combined on the drum. You will be using fine nylon, and some reserve of line is your only insurance against breakage when you hook some heavy fellow.

The cast should be nine feet in length and tapered down to 1½ or 2 lb. Breakages then occur in the weakest part of the cast – the lowest link – and result merely in the loss of the hooks. Moss and algæ are most flourishing when water is at summer level and light penetrates freely to the bottom, and as a result snagging is rather frequent; the way in which a Pennell tackle will cling to a moss-covered stone is remarkable. The tapered cast, with its fine point, soon snaps under a firm pull, and this is quite an advantage when one prefers to lose a hook tackle rather than disturb good water by wading up to free it. In fishing for the usual run of stream trout I use 1½ lb. points and casts of the natural or misty blue colour. In my opinion tinted nylon, whether green or brown, is more conspicuous in strong light and thin water than that having the usual smoky tint. Glisten matters less; it can hardly be perceptible to fish in the seethe and bubble of fast water.

We have so far considered the various items in the order in which they would be put together at the waterside if we were about to fish – rod, reel, line, cast – and so, lastly, we come to hooks. Here I am going to interrupt the sequence. The question of hook types, shapes and sizes is an extremely important one – so important indeed that I propose to devote a whole chapter to its discussion.

Meanwhile, there are other items in the outfit which, if less important, are very necessary. If you have had to curb your desire to make everything as light as possible in the matter of selecting a rod, you may be cheered by the simplicity of the rest of the kit. It consists of landing-net, a bag or creel, a container for bait, a cast and hook case, and a few small oddments.

The landing-net is worth the most careful choice, and it is difficult to find one type that will suit all kinds of fishing, i.e. all kinds of water. It may be that you will fish occasionally in biggish rivers where, though the water may be thin, there is a strong flow over a bottom of big stones. Whilst wading in such a water – and you are hardly likely to be able to cover it from the bank – you will need a net handle which will serve as a wading staff. It is rather a pity that you need this long handle because, since you are so close to your fish whilst wading, you do not need a long reach in order to net them and a short-handled net would serve just as well. In big rivers, however, you do require a staff, and it may as well consist of a stout landing-net handle.

But it will be an unmitigated nuisance to you on the smaller streams in which most of your fishing will be done, for here you will wade very little, if at all, and all the good that a long handle will do you will be, perhaps, to facilitate the netting of a fish over a bush or in some other awkward place. The disadvantages of the long-handled net on small waters far outweigh its occasional usefulness in situations of this kind.

I suggest, therefore, that you use one net-head, and have two handles for it. The pear-shaped wooden bows are both light and strong, and this type of net will stand up to a great deal of hard usage; the netting itself should be hardened with linseed oil dressing and rendered self-opening by the attachment of a small bullet to one of the strands in the bottom of the pouch. One of the handles, to be used on days when you fish a big water, should be of ash, about four feet six inches long, and weighted in the butt so that it finds bottom at once. At a convenient height, say six or eight inches below the top ferrule, a loop of leather may be attached to the shaft. Tackle makers do not, so far as I am aware, supply shafts so fitted, but would doubtless do so to order.

During fishing, the left hand, or perhaps I should say the free hand, is put through the loop to grasp the staff, which can then be allowed to hang from the wrist and so leave the hand free whilst baiting, etc. It is almost impossible to lose this net-cum-wading staff so long as the loop is over the wrist, but if it does drop whilst you are wading, it does not usually drift far, as the weight partly anchors the lower end.

For fishing small streams, a short handle of hollow cane is most suitable. It need not be more than two feet six inches long and should have a spring clip attached almost at the top ferrule and facing in such a direction that the net hangs butt downwards when slipped on the creel strap at your left elbow. A net that hangs head down is a perfect nuisance, since it catches in every waterside briar, usually at the most critical moments. It is a good plan to have screw ferrules fitted to *both* ends of this short net handle, and to fit one with a small rubber button which prevents the net from slipping out of your grasp when hand or shaft is wet.

Some of the folding nets are very good, and are

usually fitted with handles about three feet long, which make them quite convenient to carry, and give you a fairly long reach on occasions when you cannot get down to water level to net your fish.

I am not going to say very much about the bag or creel. The latter apart from being out-dated is a little unpopular for fly fishing, because the least extra effort in casting is inclined to bring it sliding forward, but this does not apply in bait fishing, where your movements are much more deliberate. It is true that on some waters you may be called on to clamber up and down banks and over obstacles of various kinds, and that in these circumstances the creel will frequently annoy you by slipping round, but this can be partly overcome fairly simply. You will require two brass 'D' rings, a length of light narrow leather strap, similar to that usually fitted to camera cases and having a buckle at one end and punchings in the first few inches of the other. You will also want two spring clips fitted with swivelling rings. Buckle the strap ends together and, holding the buckle, stretch the doubled strap and cut through it at the other end. To each of these raw ends stitch the ring of a spring clip. Now stitch one 'D' to your creel strap at the point where it enters the creel, and the other to the webbing at a point located just about where it crosses your lower waistcoat pocket. Clip the spring clips on your cross-strap into the 'D's' and you have a kind of brace which prevents the creel from slipping forward too often. Thus, if you habitually carry your creel, as I think most anglers do, on your left side, you will have a light strap which runs from the webbing on your left front, under your right arm, and down to the corner of the creel.

This idea originated, I believe, in America, and is not often used here. It almost eliminates the fault which, to my mind, makes the creel inferior to the bag. On the score of lightness and coolness the basket is definitely superior, and a medium-sized one, fitted with a broad webbing and the cross-strap, and a separate compartment for fish, is hard to beat for worm-fishing. It may be a little old-fashioned nowadays when bags are in such variety and so well-designed, but I much prefer it to any bag I have for warm weather fishing.

Then you require a cast case to contain a few spare casts and a dozen or so of hook tackles. You should have, also, one of those small bone disgorgers (for the safe release of venturesome small trout), and a knife and scissors. Lastly there is the container for bait.

Whatever you do avoid carrying your baits in a tin box. Sooner or later the lid of that box will stick and ultimately fly open suddenly – your baits taking the air with it! Ashore this is annoying; out in mid-stream it is nothing less than a catastrophe. Use, instead of a tin, the old-fashioned cloth bag and fasten it by a cord to the corner of your creel or bag, or to the strap. A hundred or so of worms in a handful of damp moss will keep fresh in this throughout the hottest summer day. The dangling bag is a little irritating at first, but it is better to endure it than to risk losing all the bait.

For the rest, well, travel as lightly as you can. The weather will be warm and bushes and waterside vegetation luxuriant, and the less you are burdened with equipment the happier you will be.

3

Hooks

To be satisfactory, a hook tackle for clear-water worm fishing, whatever its type – and there are several – must possess three features. First, it must hold the bait so that it looks as nearly natural as it is possible for a hooked worm to look; second, it must be fine and unobtrusive; and, third, it must hold the bait securely against washing or working off. These are essentials. An additional attribute in a good hook is simplicity in baiting.

Very few hooks or tackles qualify on all four points, and I think it may help you if I take some of those most commonly used one by one, and examine their merits and demerits in the light of my own experience. But first you should understand why the features referred to are so very necessary.

That the bait should be presented naturally is an elementary rule in worm-fishing. Worms become a part of the trouts' diet by various agencies, but most of them doubtless come into the stream via the field ditches and drains, by dropping from overhanging banks, or they may be grubbed by the trout from among marginal stones. Once in the water a worm drifts free and unhampered, tossed here and there, and always writhing and contorting as it spins in the grip of the current. To deceive the trout accustomed to taking such fare we have to use a tackle which will allow the bait to behave in a natural manner, whilst yet holding it firmly. This question of natural presentation of the bait influences much of worm-fishing procedure and the point must recur again and again in any discussion of the subject. Primarily, however, it is linked with the type of tackle used, its shape and size.

Now comes point number two. A hook which presents the bait well will not be of much avail if it is coarse and conspicuous. However lively the bait may be, however freely the shape of the tackle permits it to move, it will be of very little use if the hooks are thick and heavy. It is not possible entirely to conceal *any* hooks, if the worm is to move freely and if hooking is to be quick and certain, and what remains visible must be fine. The majority of worm tackles in common use are far too thick in the wire, and quite unsuitable for clear-water work. This fishing is one *only* for low clear-water conditions; if it is possible to use any but the very finest of tackles successfully, then conditions are those which really do not call for the skill which is the appeal of clear-water worm. The right conditions demand the very lightest tackle that is practical, and small baits. The entire craft is that of fine fishing and anything in the least clumsy must be avoided. This principle should never be forgotten.

We are concerned, in two ways, with the holding qualities of a hook. A good hook prevents the worm from working loose or from being washed off, and it also makes it difficult for fish to take the bait *in toto* without touching the hook points. Trout, in some feeding moods, are amazingly quick and can strip a lightly-mounted bait from the hooks with exasperating ease and perfect impunity. No worm tackle quite prevents this, but the best obviate it to some extent by holding the bait securely, however delicately it is mounted.

And our last point concerns simplicity in baiting. Speed is perhaps not so important for its own sake, but ease in baiting the hook is, because, though much depends on the nature of the water being fished, baits do not last long as a rule, even when they are not mutilated by gingerly biters. Limp baits are quite useless and rebaiting is therefore, bites or no bites, a frequent operation which would become tiresome if it was anything but simple. It is not, as I have suggested, a matter of speed, for the trout are not here one moment and gone the next, as they might be if they were cruising in search of surface food, but merely of ensuring that the bait can be properly mounted without a great deal of uncertain fingering.

Now, bearing these considerations in mind, let us look at some typical hook tackles.

THE 'PENNELL'

This, in my opinion, is the best tackle yet devised, for no other possesses so many good features. If the hooks are properly spaced it neither stretches nor bunches the bait, it holds it very securely and less obtrusively than any other multi-hook tackle, and it is simple to bait. It is, moreover, compact, in the sense that though a worm may be mounted on it lightly, and the hooks therefore exposed, the tackle is less subject to snagging than, say, the 'Stewart'. It is possible to use the very small baits which are usually advisable, on the 'Pennell', yet leave sufficient of the lively wriggling tail of the worm free. A 'Pennell' of the best type is illustrated in *Figure* 1. The hooks are of fine wire, in shape sneck bends, and are eyed. The top eye is, of course, used for attachment to the gut of the cast while that on the lower hook helps to some extent to retain the bait in position.

FIG. 1

For average conditions size 13 is as useful as any, though size can and should be varied to suit the weight of water and the size of the baits used. But I do not advise hooks larger than 11 or smaller than 14. They should not be more than about an inch apart (from bend to bend) and should be whipped to 1½ or 2 lb. nylon with dark red silk. They can be had on nylon which is simply passed through the eye and knotted on the shank, but I consider the whipped attachment is better. The knotting method was devised to eliminate the fraying of the whipping which sometimes occurs when a few fish have been taken on one tackle, but this is a small matter; the cost of discarding a well-used tackle now and then is trifling. The use of eyed hooks, though they are not necessary when whipping is used, is good, particularly in the top position, because it simplifies the attachment of a fresh tackle and does away with the need to keep tackles with their attached nylon.

THE 'STEWART'

Figure 2 shows one of these very popular tackles. It is perhaps a little more certain in hooking power than the 'Pennell' – a doubtful recommendation because, where the rod is in unpractised hands, it sometimes results in fatally secure hooking of undersized fish. This will happen occasionally, whatever tackle is used, but the three-hook combination is less kind to the victim than some others. Also, the third hook rather complicates baiting, especially with small worms; it must be put through the worm for partial concealment and this often takes all the lively movement out of a small bait.

FIG. 2

The whole tackle is inclined to break up and kill the worm more quickly than the 'Pennell' – its greatest fault, in my view – and it has not quite such a good entry when pitched from a distance.

Of course, these points of difference between the two tackles are slight in actual practice, and there can be no doubt that the 'Stewart' runs the 'Pennell' a very close second, and is in many ways very serviceable.

When very small baits are used the 'Stewart' should be made up of hooks not larger than size 14, but size 12 makes up into tackles which will take a bait larger than is suitable for the 'Pennell'. Here is a definite usefulness in the three-hook tackle – for baits for heavy water, or for those of the thin elastic variety which expose *too* much free tail when mounted on a 'Pennell'. For the average baits and conditions sizes 13 or 14 – sneck bends – are about right.

LARGE-PLUS-SMALL HOOK TACKLES

There are several of these, all very similar, and all presumably designed as improvements on the 'Pennell' on the one hand, and on the old single hook on the other. Most of them consist of a large hook, say size 5 or 6, in conjunction with a small one, about size 12, attached to the gut above the large one and facing the opposite way. The upper hook is provided to prevent the

FIG. 3

worm from slipping down as it would if the large hook was used alone, and the tackle may therefore be regarded as an effort to render the single hook suitable for clear-water fishing. As such it is definitely not worth while, in my opinion, because it does not and cannot eliminate the great inherent fault of the single hook, which is that it holds the worm rigidly and unnaturally.

This point I must return to in dealing with single hooks, but it may be said here that the large-plus-small hook combination, as shown in *Figure* 3, has to a slightly less extent the same faults as the single hook that it supersedes. The worm must be fully threaded on the larger hook, which is much too conspicuous to be left exposed; this is not particularly simple with small baits unless the wire of the hook is quite exceptionally fine. The most that I can say from experience of these tackles is that they are somewhat better than the single hook. Which is, I am afraid, only to damn with faint praise.

There are other two-hook tackles, one of which was that brought to my notice during the course of correspondence which followed some articles of mine in the angling press. It is illustrated in *Figure* 4, and is, I understand, known in some places as the 'Butcher'. It hardly requires description, but has one good feature –

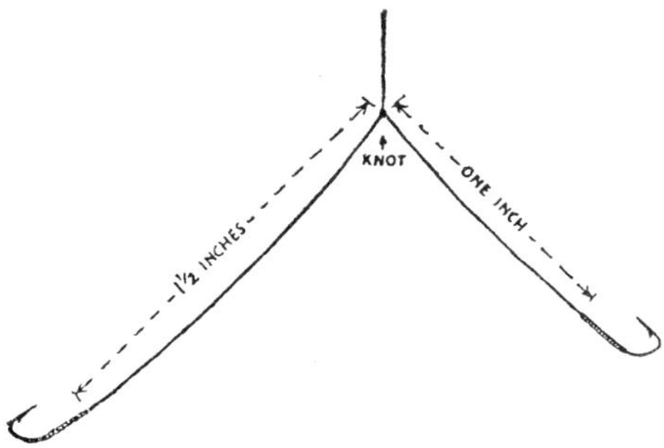

FIG. 4

the freedom it allows for movement of the bait. Otherwise it has nothing to recommend it so far as I have been able to discover by test, and has several grave faults. It is, firstly, inclined to bunch the bait when the nylon links become thoroughly twisted together. Secondly, the very small hooks which it is essential to use if they are not to be too obtrusive (the bait is lightly stitched to them and lies at right angles to the hook shanks) tend to make it very easy for the trout to pouch the bait if it is at all bunched. Lastly, as one of its sponsors naïvely suggested, the tackle nearly always hooks a trout twice – not necessarily in the mouth! I should not have thought this tackle worth mention here if I had not encountered it in use in a Welsh river some years ago, and received other indications that it has a certain popularity. It is not, apparently, in more than very local use, which is all to the good for it is surely aptly named.

THE SINGLE HOOK

The single hook is, of course, the worm tackle in its oldest and simplest form. It has, perhaps, some little advantage over multi-hook tackles in the ease with which it is baited by skilled fingers, but there its good points end so far as clear-water fishing for trout and seatrout are concerned. It is used in Ireland and in parts of Scotland in worm-fishing for salmon, but this is not clear-water work in the true sense of the term.

As I suggested when speaking of the large and small hook combination, the single hook holds the bait much too stiffly, the centre portion of the worm being rigidly curved, while the ends only are free to move. This must happen if a worm is *threaded* on a hook, and there is no other way of concealing a large or comparatively large single hook. A small single hook, on the other hand, will either fail to take hold or, again, is too easily swallowed with the bait by fish of any size from parr upwards. More than this, the single hook, because it must be threaded, kills the bait quickly and as a rule soon allows it to slip down into the position where its imply dangles on the bend of the hook.

If the single hook had any marked advantage over other types, its use might be sound enough, but it has not. Its obtrusiveness as we have seen, brings its own problem – the need for threading the bait round the bend and up the shank, to conceal the iron, a procedure quite unnecessary except for this object. The small hooks of the 'Pennell' and 'Stewart' tackles, which are put *through* the bait, hold it just as securely for all practical purposes, and a great deal more effectively. Where fish are shy – and almost all trout are shy in low clear water – the single hook is useless, lacking in hooking power, and will fail to turn to advantage many of the half-hearted bites which so often lead to secure hooking when small sharp 'Pennells' carry the bait.

Some anglers use a special type of single hook, having a 'sliced' shank. The metal of the shank is slit and the edge of the cut turned outwards to form a kind of barb. This is an improvement on the ordinary hook as the slice helps to keep the worm from slipping down. A tiny bristle, whipped to the shank and pointing up towards the cast, has a similar effect, but this is a troublesome device which does not stand up for long to the rough usage it receives, and replacements are frequent. But the single hook, simple or improved in one way or the other, is obsolete, and that is the truth of the matter. If it *is* used, however, the size should not be larger than 9 or 10 and the shape should be a round bend.

If I have wearied you with this long and very detailed discussion of a small part of the outfit, I must plead that the hook question is vitally important. All kinds of minor difficulties arise from the use of faulty hooks, among them problems associated with the timing of the strike and with needlessly severe hooking of small fry which, being very often the boldest biters, are the bane of the worm fisher's existence. You can avoid many of these troubles if you keep in mind the several essentials which, as we have seen, go to make a good hook-tackle, and base your choice accordingly.

It is my considered opinion, after trying out all types of tackle under varying conditions, during a fairly long experience, that the 'Pennell', when made up with sneck bends, is the best of all tackles. Others have their good points, as I have tried to show, and they may have some that I do not discern. I do not, therefore, try to dissuade you from experimenting for yourself. Such experience is both useful and instructive, and though you would be unwise to persist in the use of a faulty tackle merely because you felt that it *ought* to be good, there is a great deal in having confidence in the tackle you are using and, after all, results represent the acid test.

Methods of baiting some of the tackles described are given in the following chapter and, I suggest, should be studied in conjunction with the points already raised in connection with the hooks.

4

Baits and Baiting

It is a little unfortunate that the season for worm fishing should coincide with the period when baits are most difficult to find, and the use of those which may not be quite all that we would like is, therefore, sometimes quite unavoidable. It is preferable, however, to have a limited supply of really good ones than a bagful of the wrong kind, and it is well worth going to some trouble to obtain the best.

Size and colour are extremely important. If you can secure a supply of the right variety of worm you obtain the colour; size is mainly a matter of careful selection though it is true that some of the best varieties are pretty even in size and very few of those gathered will have to be discarded later as being too large. Within reason, bearing in mind the size of the tackle, it is hardly possible to have them too small. Big coarse worms are almost useless except perhaps in heavy water where seatrout are lying – conditions that are more suitable for fly than for worm fishing.

It pays to give really close attention to this matter of size. You may at times encounter the argument that a big lure is necessary for a big trout. This theory, for theory it is, is as old as the hills and survives, I imagine, because it has the curious glibness of a catchword founded on apparent commonsense. Actually, it is a complete fallacy. You may take it as certain that the bigger (and in most cases therefore, older) a trout is, the more circumspect he is in his feeding. We must not say he is wiser – that is doubtful, but we do know that big fish develop a remarkable caution in accepting any bait or lure put before them in clear water. Perhaps, though clearly they must consume a much greater volume of food than their smaller fellows, they are simply more critical of its quality. However that may be, the fact, as it concerns our subject, is that the best class of trout and seatrout will almost invariably accept a small or medium-sized worm in preference to a big one when it is offered in clear water.

The thing is soon tested if you can locate a good fish in such a situation that you are able to offer him a succession of baits without frightening him. It can be done if you take care to place the bait well upstream from his lie, and generally go about the business cautiously. The ideal site for an experiment of this kind is a bridge pool where you may be able to post a friend to peep stealthily over the parapet and note the reactions of the prospective victim.

Large worms are sometimes used in order to defeat the appalling greediness of parr and small trout, both of which eagerly attack small baits. But these little nuisances can be defeated in another way, described in Chapter Seven, without the self-imposed handicap of using big unattractive baits.

The best size of worm for the average stream is that about two and a half to three inches long; two-inch baits are, however, by no means too small. Those bigger than three inches should only be used when others are unobtainable or, on occasion, for seatrout. I did once, and only once, fish a stream – it was in the County Antrim hills – where quite small brook trout showed a decided preference for big baits. Little ones they would not have, for some obscure reason, and I made a very decent bag, fishing in gin-clear water, on four and five-inch worms obtained, after the few that I had were gone, by breaking up portions of a heavy clay bank. Incidentally on this day I had a demonstration of the amazing alertness of a feeding trout.

My bait was drifting down a very shallow fast run apparently devoid of any cover when, from beneath a fringe of trailing grasses a full six feet away from the bait, appeared a good trout. He shot across the current, making a perceptible wake, seized the worm, and surged back again in a twinkling. That fish – he was a plump well-fed fellow of nearly a pound and three-quarters and a perfect giant for the water – saw the bait dancing in a jabble of short waves from that distance!

But to return to the bait question.

In some parts of Scotland the brandling is regarded as the best bait of all, and it has a good reputation pretty generally. I am rather inclined to believe that it lives on a reputation given it by some of the older writers – Stewart had great faith in it and says, 'We hold this worm in great repute; it can be scoured in a day or two and is then a beautiful worm in appearance.' Well, that may be. For my part I have never met anyone who could offer any proof whatever of the brandling's alleged superior attractiveness, though in many places it is used more confidently than any other bait. And, of course, if a bait is fished constantly and confidently it will take fish and maintain its reputation. The brandling is easily identified by the closely-set yellowish rings which mark it and by the horrible-smelling moisture which exudes when the hooks are put through it. It is found principally in old manure heaps, and under them. It is most unpleasant to handle, is very easily broken, and is not nearly so deadly as some other worms. I started, many years ago, with immense confidence in the brandling, became puzzled and disappointed, and, finally, very curious. My ultimate conclusion, after season upon season of intermittent but patient trial of this so strangely-renowned bait, is given above.

From the poorest of the worms which are of any use at all for fishing, let us turn to the best – the 'button-worm'. This worm has the general appearance of a small lob, having a dark head and being very often found knotted into a little ball. It is sometimes rather bluish when freshly dug, but soon becomes a better colour in moss. It is common in the right size – about three inches long, or slightly less – and is lively and attractive to the trout when mounted. Poultry runs, hard beaten pathways and hard and clayey ground, are likely places in which to find button worms, but I get my supplies, as a rule, in firm old meadow-land, often whilst digging up the ragwort for the big fat white grubs that drill the roots of this plant. These grubs, by the way, are very deadly baits for trout when fished upstream like the worm. If you want to try them, here is a tip which will save you quite a little work. Look for the ragwort plants with yellow leaves; those that are dark green in colour and patently healthy seldom harbour the grubs, and it is waste of time and energy to dig them up. In digging, do not touch the plant itself, because your 'game' is in the hollow root or stem and goes back into the soil with astonishing speed immediately the stem is grasped. Simply insert the spade or fork and turn plant, root and turf over. Then break the turf away and in most cases you will find your bait. Farmers are only too pleased as a rule to allow you to attack the ragwort in their fields if you put the turf back into place.

In July and August you will find that almost every sere-looking plant harbours one of the grubs which are by the way, the larvæ of the Frosted Orange Moth. They do not keep very well, but will live for a few days in a box with a few stems or roots of rag-wort.

Of the worms, the second in order of usefulness is the red worm. It varies a good deal in size but is easily recognized by its bright colour and liveliness. In rich soils it is, I think, the commonest worm, but I find it most abundant, in any district, in garden refuse heaps, grass-cuttings and in very rich vegetable debris. You are almost certain to find a few red worms under old dry cattle droppings in the fields. It is rather more difficult to harden up than the button worm and is inclined to be fragile and to break on baiting. The trout of small low-land streams are particularly fond of this worm, which is as well, since it is sometimes – when weather is very dry – the only bait you can find in any quantity.

The marsh worm is common almost everywhere. You will find numbers if you leave a flat piece of wood on the grass for a week or two, to hold the moisture. Under stones, in moist earth generally, beneath garden rubbish heaps – these are the places in which to look for the marsh worm, which is pale and sometimes carries a white band above the tail. It is a worm that I seldom use, in spite of its commonness, because of its softness and tendency to break up on the hook.

A medium-sized lob is sometimes a good bait for sea-trout before they become stale and shy, but willingness to take a largish worm often implies a boldness which would surely bring them up to the fly if it was offered them, and I therefore consider that worm-fishing in such circumstances is somewhat out of place and hardly worth more than passing mention.

Most worms, when freshly dug, are anything but suitable for immediate use. Their internal economies are full of soil and they are dark-coloured and soft. Since you want them to be the reverse – well and clearly coloured and tough – something has to be done. You should first find a cool shady corner in outhouse or garden where you can keep a deep box or earthenware crock. I use one of the old-fashioned earthenware bread crocks, mainly because it keeps its contents cooler and moister than a box. A thick timbered box, however, will do quite well as will, in fact, any box which is stout enough to resist warping and gaping at the corners, and deep enough to keep its contents moist. You should half-fill your jar or box with moss; any moss will do so long as it is not the green velvety stuff that grows on walls, or that which grows on submerged stones. I have used moorland mosses of several kinds – which I am not botanist enough to name, but the best is the feathery variety found on old trees and among the woodland ferns. The moss should be put into the box slightly damp.

Turn your freshly-dug worms out on top of it and pick off any damaged ones and any lumps of soil. Some writers recommend washing the worms, and Stoddart said that they should then be permitted to crawl about on a dry board! This is taking it to absurd lengths and you need not attempt either to launder your baits or to marshal them on a board. They will clean themselves perfectly by working down through the moss, but you must be sure that the latter is well pressed down on the bottom so that the worms do not gather on the bare wood in a muddy mass of their own casts. Every few days you should turn the moss over and pick out any dead or weakly baits. Do not attempt to feed them on cream, as some people will advise you to do; it only turns sour and nasty. You can sprinkle brickdust among the moss if you like, it improves the colour of the baits to some slight extent.

You should fit your 'wormery' with a lid heavy enough to fit closely by its own weight, and have it pierced round and about the centre for ventilation. In a store place of this kind worms will keep for weeks, but you must remember to look at them occasionally and take out casualties, or you will lose them all. Replenish your stock from fresh diggings as you draw on it, and do not hesitate to go to some trouble to obtain the best. You cannot go far wrong in your choice if you remember that the ideal bait, whichever kind of worm is used, should be red or pink, reasonably tough, and, above all, lively. Trout will not take flabby limp baits and if you fish them you merely waste good water and your time. The quality of the bait makes all the difference. Over and over again I have found that a change to a fresh lively worm will result in a fish from a place whence there came no sign of a bite whilst I used a limp or sodden bait, but where I felt sure a fish must be lying.

Having expended much careful consideration on the selection of both hook-tackle and baits, you must know how to make use of them in a way that will exploit their best qualities. Here are the points to be watched. The bait must look natural and be free to wriggle and twist about. It must be held securely but so lightly that it does not shield the hook points and militate against firm hooking. You will, I hope, forgive reiteration here of points already made when discussing hooks. It is necessary that they should be remembered in *using* the hooks.

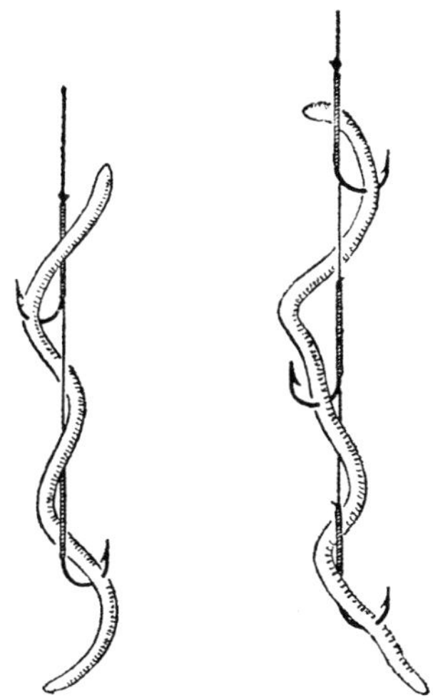

FIG. 5

To bait the 'Pennell' tackle, insert the upper hook about a third of the bait's length from the head, bringing the barb right through. If the bait is of the restless, elastic variety, the upper hook can be put through twice, making a loop in the bait. The lower hook is treated similarly and the tail of the worm left free to wriggle as it will. On no account break the bait if it is too long for the tackle. It is better to loop it as described, or to twist it once or twice round the nylon after inserting the first hook and before impaling it on the second. It will work out the twists in some mysterious fashion before long, but it will then be time to discard it and mount a fresh one. The 'Stewart' tackle is baited similarly, except, of course, that the worm is fastened in three places. I have heard objections raised on the question of leaving the tail of the worm free. It is said that the trout nip off this portion without touching the hooks. This is true, but it only occurs if and when the fish have time fully to inspect the bait – a thing that rarely happens. The lively, wriggling tail, on the other hand, is the most attractive part of the bait; if it is hooked up its value in this respect is nil.

Figure 5 shows baited 'Pennell' and 'Stewart' tackles.

If the baits are soft and easily broken it may be advisable not to put the hooks through but merely to thread the points under the skin, bringing them out about an eighth of an inch farther along. Thus the bait is lightly stitched to the hooks. This is quite sound practice at any time. It is not sound, however, to conceal the points of either upper or lower hooks in the bait; the barbs should be clear always. If you do not bring them through, the bait will work off the hooks almost at once. And quite apart from this, the tough skin of a well-seasoned bait can shield the hook points quite effectively and cost you any number of shyly-biting fish.

The large-plus-small hook combination is baited by inserting the large hook far enough from the head of the bait to allow of the latter being threaded on until the hook shank is covered. The point is then brought through. The tail of the worm is brought round and impaled on the upper and smaller hook. See *Figure* 6. The bait must be mounted similarly when the plain single hook is used.

It will be seen that whereas in the case of the 'Pennell' and 'Stewart' tackles the worm is mounted head towards the cast, i.e. pointing up the line, with the large hooks it hangs head downwards. The reason is this. The head of the worm is tougher than the tail and the latter would break if it were threaded and pierced by the comparatively thick wire of the large hook. So, when this type of tackle is used, the tougher portion of the worm is threaded on. With the tackles made up of small hooks this does not arise, and the head of the worm goes on the

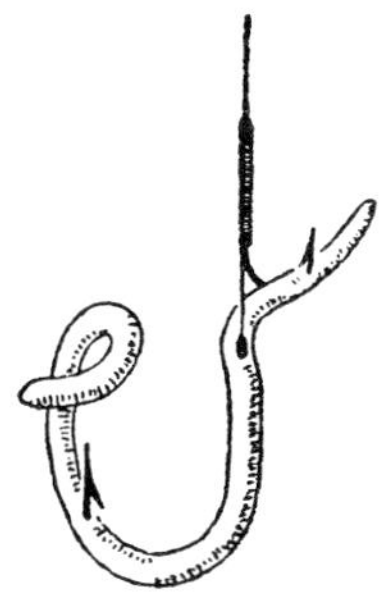

FIG. 6

top hook, partly because one instinctively impales the thicker and firmer portion first, on the top hook, and partly because it is not so easy for a trout to steal a bait so mounted as it is when the head is on the lower hook. The tail is most likely to break away at any time and, of course, if this happens when a bait is hooked head downwards, the whole length of the bait simply dangles from the lowest hook and is easily taken. But a bait dangling by the tough head, from the upper hook, is a different proposition.

I do not think that trout designedly take a worm either head or tail first, nor that there is anything in the way of baiting a tackle, from this point of view. Using the 'Pennell' you will find that most fish have obviously taken the bait tail first, but in my opinion this has no significance beyond pointing to the fact that a bait mounted head uppermost drifts more or less in that position due to the slight lifting influence of the upwardly inclined nylon of the cast. The head of the bait is not so much heavier than the tail that it will sink against the pull of the cast.

Some years ago I made some experiments with small trout in an aquarium in an attempt to see whether there was any marked consistency in their way of accepting worms thrown in. There was none. As a rule the fish dashed at the worm and seized it by what was presumably the most convenient part! Sometimes the worm was swallowed tail first and sometimes by the head, and often it was taken by the middle. I often saw the trout negotiating a worm held across the jaws as a pike holds a small fish. The liveliest worms were always taken first and a dead or nearly dead one would be nosed and pushed about and, eventually, left lying. These trout were kept in a tank in a quiet outhouse and were as wild as could be, so that the experiments, such as they were, may have served as some slight indication of what happens in the stream.

Here, to end this chapter, is a 'don't'. Don't, as I have several times seen advised in print, stun the bait by giving it a sharp tap in the palm of your hand. It may make it easier to put on the hooks, but it spoils it for fishing. A good bait may be wriggling and elusive and awkward to hold, but that is all to the good. The livelier it is the better.

5

When and Where to Fish

WORM fishing begins some time about the middle of June, or when trout have ceased to rise to the fly with the readiness they show in April and May. Everything depends upon weather, of course, but in a *normal* season you can begin to fish the worm in the third week in June and carry on until the middle of August. July is the best month as a rule all over the country. Trout are then markedly shy of anything artificial in the fly line, and the only time offering any chance of success is after sunset. The rivers are dead low and crystal clear and half the anglers of your acquaintance are mooning about waiting for a change in the weather, or the arrival of the weekly fishing papers, and reading about other people's catches in other parts. This is the time to fish the worm.

Of course, though it has happened rarely within recent years, there may be rain and floods, or water just too high without being in flood, for days on end, in July. The rivers are up and down by turns and the fish thoroughly unsettled, or they may not feed with any readiness owing to sultry dull weather. Except possibly in the conditions last mentioned, the fly is more suitable than the worm.

To fish the worm as it should be fished, you should

go out in warm bright weather when the barometer is settled and streams perfectly clear and low. When such conditions have held for a day or two, trout are fairly distributed over the available water.

Wind is not necessary for sport, though an upstream breeze does help you to fish the more slowly flowing water and certain flats that would be unapproachable without ripple. The point is not important, however, because the whole essence of upstream worm fishing is the exploitation of running water and a travelling bait. If you fish really flat water – granting that a breeze makes it possible to approach it – you descend perilously near to 'worm-drowning', for the bait must rest idly and half the charm of the game, its need for unflagging alertness, is lost. There is one way of fishing *deep* still pools that is interesting, but we shall come to that presently.

Ninety per cent of worm fishing covers only fast or comparatively fast water and, in consequence, you need not hesitate to fish when the sun is blazing down from a cloudless sky and in the dead water you can see every pebble on the bottom. These conditions are good.

So much for the kind of day required, and now for the time of day. You can really fish all through a summer day with some chance of success, but there are certain hours which are better than others and there are, sometimes, quite sharply-defined 'takes'. The best time of all is from about sunrise to nine or ten a.m. In the early morning trout are feeding in earnest, though fishing is more difficult, owing to the fact that fish are widely scattered in the thinnest water where special care is necessary in approach. As the sun rises higher, fish become harder to find, because a fair proportion of them is moving back into daytime hovers in the deeper pools.

For some reason which has always eluded me, I have found that the white grub found in the ragwort roots, and mentioned in the section dealing with baits, is particularly deadly in the sunrise hour. This by the way.

One thing is fatal to early morning sport, and that is mist. Trout will not take until it has been dissipated by the sun.

The early part of the day, i.e. from sunrise to noon, is much the best and if you have not done well by noon you have little chance of saving the day. Fish sometimes seem to regain a little of their early keenness for food about noon or just before, but this 'take' does not last long and is not to be depended on. The afternoon, and evening up to within a couple of hours of sunset are not good, except perhaps on small hill streams where trout are not nearly so capricious – possibly owing to their perpetual hunger on the short commons that a mountain burn usually affords!

The evening between sunset and dusk (and afterwards if you want to fish on – but this is not clear-water fishing!) is very good indeed, but not quite so good as the early morning. The movements of the trout are now in the reverse direction – they are moving out of the pools and deeper holes and are spreading out in the thin water of the flats, in the pool tails, and generally into situations that may be described as 'night-lies'. Their after-dusk feeding positions have not the same relation to shelter and the other things which go to make up good holding-places, that the day-time lies have, and many fish are hovering or cruising here and there in the most exposed places as the light fails.

You will find that, whatever the time of day, a readiness to take the worm is often signalized by a general rise to natural fly. If trout are on the lookout for food and are willing to rise, they will usually take the worm if you can present it to them, but I do not think that this applies with quite the same force during the afternoons of those heavy airless days which seem to produce such enormous hatches of midges or smuts. Trout feeding on these very tiny flies will not take bait any more readily than they will rise to artificial fly, wet or dry. At most other times you may hope to take a few fish from among those rising, however uncatchable they may be to the man fishing fly. That, at least, is my experience.

Much more might be said about the feeding-times of trout, but I feel that in indicating the hours likely to prove best on the average stream I have gone as far as is wise. No two streams are quite alike so far as the habits of their trout are concerned, and it is rare to find conditions quite constant in any stream for more than a day or two at a time. In the circumstances, useful conclusions can only be drawn from study of local conditions and from personal observation, and I cannot emphasize too strongly the wisdom of taking careful note of feeding-times and their accompanying conditions in light, temperature and height of water. These govern the activity of the food of the trout and of the trout themselves, and, subject to variation according to season, produce similar results whenever they recur. When conditions do not produce the result we have learnt to associate with them, we may feel tolerably certain that there is a subtle difference between what we have seen in the past, and the superficially similar state of affairs before us. It is recognition of this difference that marks the really observant angler, who, from his store of rivercraft, unearths some kind of parallel which, if providing no solution of the problem itself, at least indicates a reasoned plan of action. No book can ever help the angler in this way; experience is the only qualified instructor.

I have suggested, thus far, the season, weather conditions and times of day most suitable for worm-fishing, and now we must look at the kind of water we need.

Most upland streams carry plenty of good worming water. This does not necessarily consist of shallow reaches which are certain to hold trout, for your problem is not so much to find the fish – you are bound to do that if you fish *any* water thoroughly – but to find the lies whose occupants you have a chance of deceiving; to find the spots where the current will help to conceal your tackle and give life to the drifting bait. You want ripple and movement and where you find plenty of it you have good worming water.

You can pass over the long, still, shallow flats common to rivers of the type of the headwaters of some Lancashire and Yorkshire rivers, unless they are well bushed and you can stalk risers and drop the bait in their rise rings. This very chancy business saves this type of water from utter uselessness, for it cannot be fished in the ordinary way. The fish in such places are usually baskers or little fellows whose chief function, it would seem, is to dash off upstream, spreading alarm among their fellows. Besides, as I have said elsewhere in this chapter, you must fish these still flats with a stationary bait – dreary procedure at the best. Flat water which is deep offers a better chance of taking fish, and trout can be taken on worm in the slowly-flowing deep class of river. But this is not clear-water worm fishing at all, for the bait lacks the brisk movement which induces sharp biting in the trout, and the need for constant concentration on the angler's part.

The use of worm is clearly and definitely limited to more or less fast-flowing rivers and burns; elsewhere it is both out of place and useless from the point of view of the sport it affords.

But it must not be thought that the deep water, naturally slower in flow than shallow, should be ignored, merely because of its depth. In Scotland and Ireland there are countless rivers, some of them of considerable size, where deep pools alternate with short stretches of thinner water. There is a certain technique in fishing these deep pools, and they are not in the same category as the canal-like stretches of deep slowly-flowing rivers referred to above. Where deep water consists of pools, as distinct from dead flat reaches, there is always a perceptible run of water which can be exploited and there is always movement of the bait without aid from the rod.

Again, speaking of deep water, there is a type of stream which, in dry weather, becomes a succession of deep rocky holes linked by narrow, gushing channels, or miniature falls. You can fish worm in hill waters of this kind, and very successfully too, if you are careful to introduce the bait by way of the inflow or by dropping it in quietly at the head.

The ideal clear-water worming river or stream is that which is, as a whole, shallow, with few flats and plenty of streamy pools of medium depth; the type of water which has a scattering of boulders on the briskly-flowing shallows, partially bushed banks, and a course that twists and turns through fertile upland pastures, should provide first-class sport.

In low water ideal for upstream worm though cover for the angler is limited

Cover totally absent and approach very difficult

Not all of it will prove productive, however, and your plan of action must be varied to exploit the best of it. Accordingly, it is important, in fishing any stream, that you should be able to 'size up' any piece of water, to assess its possibilities and to decide where trout are most likely to be lying. You will, naturally, try to fish every foot of the water, but with your short line you must inevitably spoil some of it in reaching the rest. You cannot use a long line to reach distant water as you could if you were using fly. It pays you, therefore, to be able to make a discerning preliminary survey and to plan your approach to each small section of stream with the object of fishing the most promising portions of it from the best and least conspicuous quarters. This can present quite a problem when you have to approach by wading up in thin water.

The whole question of making the most of your water turns on your ability to recognize 'holding-places' when you study the part you are about to fish. It is a faculty that grows in one. With experience and careful observation the thing becomes, or can become, almost an instinct. I do not think it is more than that. Positive knowledge cannot enter into it in the sense that any man can say with certainty, 'Today trout will be in that run,' or 'We shall find them in the pool and *only* there . . .' Nor can anyone say that a particular spot is certain to be occupied by a trout, or conversely, that that spot is untenanted. Occasionally the prophet might be right, but more often this kind of confidence is misplaced. 'Trouty' looking water is often all but useless and 'hopeless' water the best of all. It pays to distrust the appraisal *of the eye alone* and to remember past experiences, successes and failures, and weather conditions, and everything that makes up a kind of instinct which will prompt you to the wisest course more often than mere rule of thumb.

In summer and at certain times of the day trout may be anywhere; they are frequently in the most unexpected and surprising places.

Yet there is something – one constant factor – which, however mysterious the whereabouts and behaviour of trout may be at times, can be taken into account in making your appraisal of the positions of fish and the prospects of presenting your bait to them, in any water. This is the fact, obvious enough in a way, that the necessity to find food is the strongest influence there is in the trout's existence. Most of its time and energy are spent in the pursuit of food. Trout gravitate naturally to those points where food is most plentiful, and although in a south-country stream such a point may well consist of, say, a weed-patch rich in insect food, in upland waters it is much more likely to be a spot specially rich in food owing to the set of the current that washes it, rather than to the food-producing qualities of its immediate surroundings.

The things to be studied, therefore, in deciding which portions of a stretch of river are worth special attention, are the direction and strength of the flow and the contour of the stream bed. Where their joint influence results in a concentration of water-borne food – in suspension or deposited on the bottom – there the trout are most likely to be found. To this extent, then, there is a feature common to all trout lies.

In the low water conditions suitable for worm-fishing, most feeding trout are located, as a rule, at or near the broken water at the pool head. They often lie on the shelving lip of the pool, where the fast water is flattening down, and in the corners of the hole on both edges of the streamy part. Another favourite lie is also on the edges of the current, but lower down where its strength is waning and drifting food (and your bait) sink slowly to the bottom. A bait drifting out of faster water into one of these quiet spots will be taken readily often enough, but if placed directly into quiet water in the first instance will be refused. Herein lies the difference between baits presented naturally and unnaturally.

Rocks or boulders that create a quiet pocket on their downstream sides often harbour trout, but not so often as is popularly supposed. Food undoubtedly collects there, but the eddy is often too strong for the place to be a comfortable lie for fish. An accumulation of driftwood and rubbish about the obstruction will, however, make such a place a 'sure find'. The driftwood often throws the eddies farther out and forms a really quiet retreat for a trout. A low undercut bank, particularly if it borders the deeper side of a fast-running pool, or if the incoming flow strikes it at an angle, is probably the finest holding-place of all. Seatrout especially like it.

Where banks are sandy or crumbling and are given to breaking away in turf-crowned sections, to topple down into water which more or less covers them, you will often find that the watery crevasses thus formed close to the bank hold fish. On one Scottish river that I know these bank-falls provide some of the most productive water – a fact which I discovered quite by accident, and in very pleasant fashion, by taking a two-pound seatrout from a hole into which I had idly swung the bait. Since then I have taken many trout and some seatrout from similar places which, for some reason, usually

Two stretches of river
ideal for fishing the upstream worm

shelter fish of a very good class. Unfortunately, these bank-falls are commonest where banks are high and bare and they are consequently difficult to approach unless the water below is shallow.

Along the smaller streams which flow through low ground, the banks are often much overgrown with long grasses, meadowsweet and similar straggling vegetation, and where this stuff trails in the water or overhangs is generally a good lie for trout. So, too, is the edge of a watercress-bed or clump of mimulus, the hole beneath a willow or alder root, or in the shade of any low-hanging bush. In the Scottish lowlands it is a common practice, when bridging a burn, to put down a kind of pavement of rough setts in the bed of the stream beneath the bridge. There may be only three or four inches of water flowing over such a sunken causeway, but it is a place of which trout are very fond, and always deserves careful fishing.

Small burns of the moorland and mountain class are rather different; the places that hold trout in them are more open. Hollow peat banks are, occasionally, worth special attention, but in my experience trout are not very keen on these bare caverns, unless they are directly in the run of the current. Most of the fish lie about mid-stream boulders, in rock clefts, little runnels out of the main current, or right in the white water if and where it covers large stones with gaps between them.

These are some of the places which should be viewed as likely holding-places, but there are many others, and just as there is no end to the variety of streams, so there is no end to the diversity of places where trout will be found at some time and under some conditions. Your tactics for each pool should enable you to make the most of the best water, and to pass over none of the little corners that might conceivably hold a fish.

In particular, do not disdain to fish very thin water, whatever the type of stream in which it occurs. You will often find trout on the edge of gravelly shallows where there is barely enough water to conceal them. You will never cease to marvel at the number of unlikely apparently thoroughly unpromising spots that can hold trout. In fact, until you are experienced on any water, you will add considerably to your bag during the worm-fishing season if you make a point of fishing every place of which you are inclined to say at sight, 'Well, there won't be a trout *there*!'

But – and it is a very big 'but' – do not go out of your way to follow out this Irishman's rule. Never waste what you have reason to think is good water in order to reach that of which you have any doubt.

6

How to Fish

THOUGH you may evolve a method of your own in getting the bait out and may, as indeed you should, vary your procedure to suit the surroundings and the elbow-space available at each run or pool, there is one rule to which you must adhere very strictly. You must always fish upstream whenever possible.

It may happen that you are forced to fish across sometimes, because an obstacle on your side – an outgrowing bush, for instance – prevents you from fishing up to a lie beyond it, but even here you should try to observe the rule and, in effect, fish upstream by taking care that your rod-point is below the bait. Only thus can you strike downstream.

The principal reason why you must fish up is, of course, that only by doing so are you able to approach fish lying in low clear water unseen. The need for a downstream strike is an important factor, as is too the fact that the bait must travel quite unhindered. If you fished downstream the bait would come to the top as soon as the line straightened, and there make a wake like a speed-boat. Trout will not take a bait which is behaving like this, and even if they would you could hook only a small percentage of those that offered.

In addition to fishing always upstream to avoid detection, you will find it necessary at times to adopt other precautions in approaching your water – to crawl along the water's edge, below the skyline on open banks, to wade – bent like the oldest inhabitant – along the margin of the shallows, to wade, half-crouched, in midstream – all according to background. And you should be able to place your bait accurately by the means I shall presently describe, whilst in all manner of inconvenient attitudes.

The preceding chapter in some respects overlaps this one, but I have chosen to treat the handling of the rod and the placing and control of the bait as a separate branch of the subject for the sake of clarity. The close association, in their effect on worm-fishing technique, between fishable and 'fishy' water and the means of access to it, is apparent at every point.

And now to the actual handling of the rod; in this I think we may well start, as we do at the beginning of a day's fishing, with the assembly of rod and tackle. In fixing the reel to the rod, place it so that when the end button of the rod rests against your forearm just in front of your elbow, it (the reel) hangs below your wrist. Here it is convenient, out of the way, and balances a rod of the description and weight suggested in Chapter Two very well indeed. If your rod has a fixed reel seating, the reel may be farther back, but it does not matter very much.

Rod up and line threaded, attach an eyed 'Pennell' to the cast and loop the cast to the line. If you fish, as I advise you to do, without using a bite-indicator and without shot to weight the cast, you are now ready to bait your tackle and begin. Opinion is divided on the question of using shot; the point is an important one, and I shall deal with it more fully presently.

The bite-indicator is a small device which is not necessary, but may be used to some advantage during your first essays in worm fishing. It consists of a small piece – say about three-quarters of an inch long – of fine white quill, or an inch of white cotton or floss silk, which is knotted to the cast about three feet from the hooks. It is easier to detect the slight hesitation in the drift of the line, the momentary arrest that may be the sign of a bite, by this device, especially if you find unfaltering concentration on the fine cast something of an eye-strain. Until you become used to watching the movement of the nylon at the point where it enters the water, the little white tell-tale is an asset, but you must not get into the habit of relying on it to indicate the bites. If you do this, you may be inclined to forget always to keep a tight line.

But we must go back to the moment when we had imagined you ready to fish.

Now, whether you propose to fish from the bank or by wading, you will have decided, from your preliminary survey of the water immediately ahead as you look upstream, which of the several promising spots within 'casting' distance you will try first. Get down to water level or as near it as possible, if you cannot or do not wish to wade, a little way downstream, and work cautiously up until you think you are in a position to put the bait slightly beyond your objective.

The act of placing the bait is always more or less of a pitching movement, i.e., an underhand rather than an overhand 'cast', but there are three variations in the *commencement* of a cast. You may hold the bait in the left hand as it is held in making the switch and catapult 'casts', you may begin with the bait swinging loosely, or you may catch it up in a finger of your rod hand. Let us see how the first method works out in actual practice.

Draw off about a foot more than a rod length of line, take the cast, a few inches above the bait, between thumb and forefinger of your left hand, and with your right lift the rod up on a partially extended arm till your left hand feels the pull of the line and the rod tip is slightly bowed. Now bring your rod hand and arm, and the rod, back, following with the left hand, which comes towards the right so that the bait is held nearly under the rod. Next, urge the rod slightly forward and upward rather smartly, at the same instant releasing your hold on the cast. This, though it sounds absurdly complicated for a very simple series of movements, describes the switch 'cast'. It is the easiest way to get a bait out.

The bait should travel straight to the spot aimed at, alighting there with the minimum of splash. If you think that the 'cast' – I quote the word here and elsewhere because it is not a cast in the true sense of the word – is a bad one and threatens to spoil the water, you can arrest the flight of the bait quite simply by halting the rod in its 'follow-through'. Do not, however, flip the bait back or you may find yourself in trouble owing to banks or trees behind you.

Never look down at the bait or the butt of the rod at the moment of release. Fix your eyes on the place where you want the bait to fall. You will find that the bait and the upper part of the rod come into view so quickly and in such a manner that the whole process is one of taking aim – a process that becomes less of conscious effort and more and more of easy accuracy with practice.

Now we must consider an alternative way of getting the bait out – this time using only one hand. Whilst wading in a big water you need the left hand free to handle the wading staff and, quite apart from this, in fishing one possible lie after another in quick succession up a thickly-populated stretch of water, it is both unnecessary and a waste of time for you to recover the line into the left hand each time you make a fresh throw. Your whole procedure, apart from re-baiting, is a one-hand business unless, because of obstacles or a troublesome wind, you are forced to use the switch 'cast', or the catapult 'cast' described later. So, in repetition 'casting' over a long reach of open water, the bait is allowed to swing idly between throws.

A little experience will bring you an increasing deftness in manipulating the light and freely-swinging bait, in giving it the forward urge by using the simple pitching movement which is the basis of all the 'casts' used in open water fishing.

The single-handed 'cast' may be commenced in two ways; the bait can be free, or it can be held inside a hooked finger of the rod hand. Before I describe the 'cast' itself I should emphasize the usefulness of this last little dodge. Its principal virtue is that it saves much trouble whilst you are fishing in badly-treed places, in a gusty wind, or otherwise in conditions that render it unwise to allow the bait to swing free between 'casts'.

I suggest, therefore, that you start from the beginning to cultivate the habit of swinging the bait back into your rod grip and there hooking a finger round the nylon, at times when you are not actually fishing. In any case, you will have to examine the bait before 'casting' again, wherever there has been a distinct

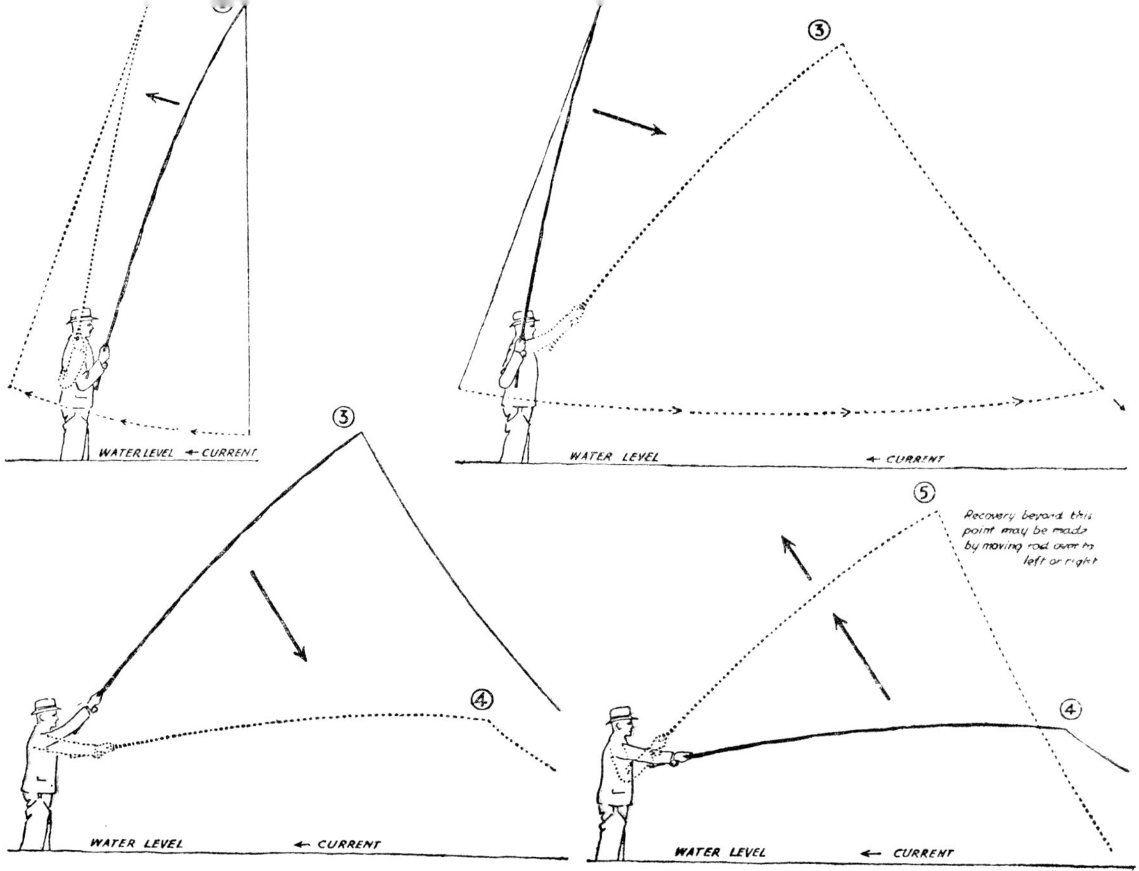

FIG. 7 The movements of the swing 'cast'

interval since your last throw, and you will have to swing it back to your hand for this purpose. This recovery of the bait after each 'cast' in badly obstructed water, or when you move your position more than a few steps between casts, soon becomes a habit and may even be found a definite aid to accurate placing of the bait. I often think that the latter, released by the straightening of the finger at the proper instant, goes straighter towards its objective than it would have done after quite a bit of preliminary swinging!

The only objection to this simple trick is that the line must be rather short and has a tendency to wrap itself round the rod-tip. The jerking imparted to the rod as you wade on a rough bottom or negotiate rough banks causes the line to flip over the rod – an annoying occurrence, not always noticed until you try to make a fresh 'cast', and find that the line does not lead from the end ring.

When you commence with the bait swinging loose, the action of casting is as follows. The rod is held almost vertically on a partly extended arm so that the bait hangs before you and a few feet away. The rod-arm and rod are then drawn back bodily in order to increase the length of the bait's forward swing. The latter is imparted by a smooth but quick forward lift of the whole rod. The bait swings outward and as it goes towards the spot you have aimed at, the rod should follow, on your extended arm, and go downwards as the worm touches the water. *Figure* 7 illustrates the several movements in this very simple 'cast'.

In commencing with the bait hooked up to the rod-grip, the point of the rod is held somewhat lower and where the objective is at the extreme limit of your reach, may have to be dropped until it is parallel with the water. It is lifted forward and upward rather quickly so that the bait clears the water as it swings away from the hand. In this 'cast' you must guard against a too-sharp flip in the lifting movement or you will find that the bait goes up and not out!

At the moment when the bait reaches the water, whichever method you adopt to get it there, you must check the dip of the rod and raise the top to take up the slack which begins to develop in the gut as soon as the current grips the bait.

Remember the need to be in constant touch with the bait. In fast water a bait pitched a yard or so above a possible lie may have reached that spot and been taken almost before you have got the rod up again. From the beginning the line must never have been allowed to drown, or even to sag unduly between rod-tip and water-line. The importance of correcting any downward tendency of the rod after the bait is in the water can, therefore, hardly be over-stressed. Only in this way can you defeat the good fish that strip the tackle cunningly, and the little fellows who would swallow it beyond anything but surgical recovery operations.

The point is, briefly, that you cannot either detect or analyse any bite unless your line is straight. Your analysis of bites is discussed at length in the chapter that follows, but it must be mentioned here because it bears directly upon your way of handling the line after the throw has been made and the rod raised again.

Thereafter you should continue to raise the rod in step with the bait's drift towards you, until it is pointing, say, half-way between water and sky. Then, since its further elevation gives ever-lessening control of the bait, you must work the rod gradually over towards right or left to fish the cast out.

Your guide as to the straightness of the line is the angle formed between the cast and the surface of the stream; your rod is well-handled if you are getting a straight line without pulling on the bait. Until you can do this you will have to experiment in order to find just how much lift of the rod is necessary to avoid belly without accelerating the natural speed of the bait. You will find that both speed and direction of the bait's movement alter with almost every cast, but you must just keep the line as straight as you can.

In the normal fishing position, you should work, during all but the first moment or so of each drift down, with the reel seat under your wrist and the butt of the rod under your forearm. It is easy to fish with a twelve-foot rod for a whole day, using only one hand, in this way.

In a day's fishing your method of putting the bait quietly in the desired place (ideally not less than three or four feet above the suspected lie of a fish) may have to be varied many times to suit surroundings. You will be able to make your own adaptation of the 'casts' I have suggested to suit yourself and the needs of the moment, and it does not matter very much how ungraceful or clumsy-looking your rod movements may appear, so long as you achieve accuracy, quietness in dropping the bait, and distance. So long as these points are kept in view you can evolve your own technique, but do not use any kind of overhead cast, in any circumstances. It breaks the bait and has other bad features. The underhand 'casts' occasionally splash the bait into the water – the overhead cast always does so. Trout must consider a rain of heavily-splashing worms highly unusual, to say the least of it and, in any case, if the worm has remained intact after its express flight overhead, it soon breaks up and dies after a few splashy throws.

The catapult 'cast', already mentioned, requires a little practice, but it is extremely useful in enabling one to reach water beneath low-hanging trees, culverts and other obstacles which prevent elevation of the rod top or anything but the flattest trajectory in the bait's flight.

You can practise the catapult throw on the lawn, with the aid of a cord stretched between two trees, or a couple of chairs placed about six feet apart. The cord, to begin with, can be four feet from the ground, the height being reduced as you progress. Stand, in the first place, so that your rod, extended before you as if you were fishing, is parallel with the cord, though, of course at a higher level. You should be about a rod-length away from the cord and three or four paces from the near end. Thus, assuming that you are casting towards your right, the opening framed by the cord and its supports is well over to your right and ahead of you. Now draw off about a rod-length of line and pinch one or two small shot on the cast two feet above the bait. Hold the cast lightly but firmly between forefinger and thumb of your left hand at a point a few inches above the shot.

Lower the rod tip and draw the left hand back until the line is taut and the rod bowed with the pull. Now release your hold on the line, at the same time making a sharp back-hand cut towards your right. The movement of the rod should be checked as soon as sufficient impetus is imparted to the bait and the greater part of the rod's path is covered by what is merely a 'follow-through'. The final position of the rod, as shown in *Figure* 8, should be such as to allow the last of the slack line to go out as the bait loses momentum.

In making this 'cast' you must put rather more strain on the rod top than you do in making the 'switch' and, of course, the rod is held lower.

There are two objections to this method of getting a line out. It is difficult to do left-handed, and it calls for a very good eye for distance; the most horrible hang-up usually results from putting too much force into the 'cast'. But there is not, as I imagine you may think, any chance of straining the rod top unless you do use too much force. If you bowed the rod too far, and persisted in doing so, you might damage it, but this is hardly likely to arise because you would find that the bait was being flipped into the water with great force and you would have to be more gentle for the sake of good fishing.

The usefulness of the 'cast' far outweighs any disadvantages it may have, and it is worth studying, especially if you are likely to fish to any extent in tree-fringed streams of the lowland kind. The conditions that demand its use – such as the need to float a bait down a tunnel of arching branches – often make it difficult to keep a straight line by the usual means, i.e. raising the rod. In a case like this you should keep the rod point working round to right or left, so that you can strike downstream. Or, if the stream is narrow and you cannot turn the rod to one side or the other, you can shorten line as the bait descends by drawing it in with the left hand. Do not do this unless it cannot be avoided, however, as it tends to pull on the bait. How you can best keep the line straight is really a matter for the exercise of ingenuity, as each occasion arises. Fortunately, in the

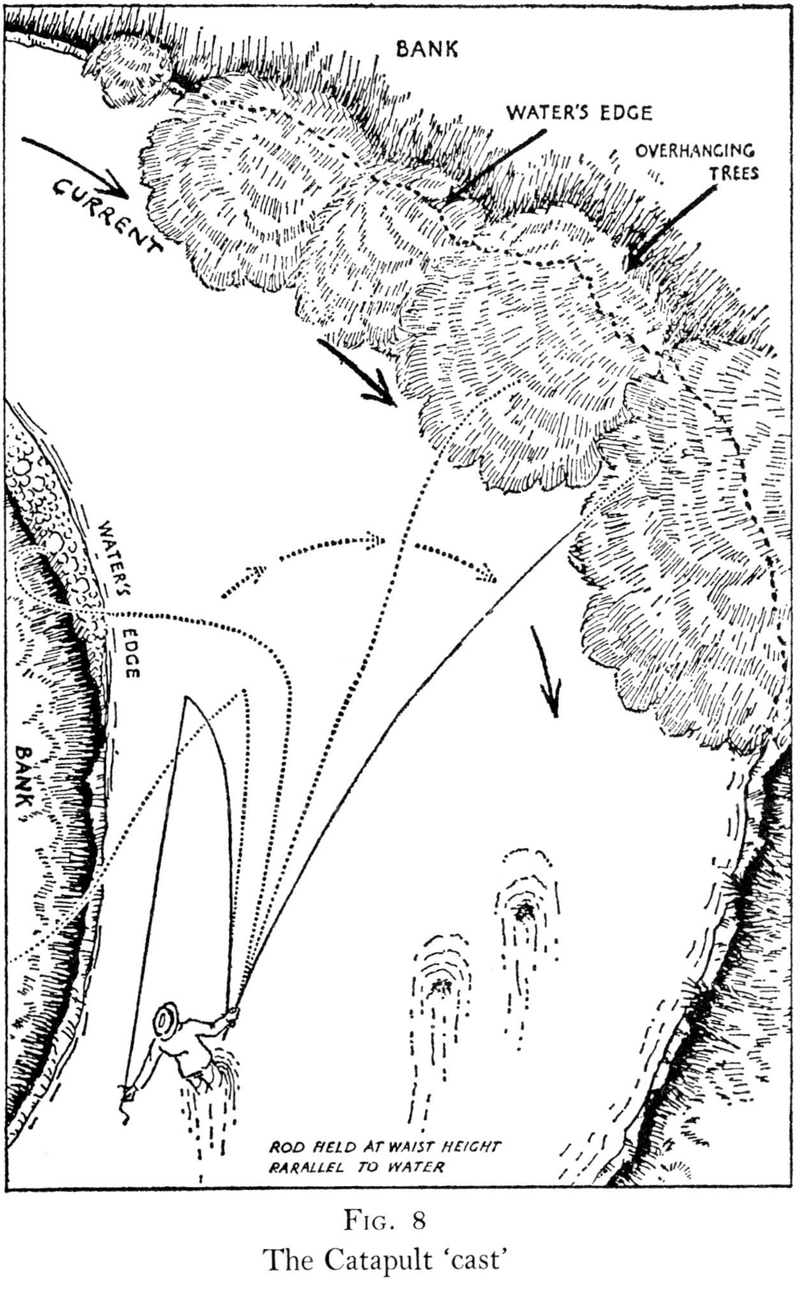

FIG. 8
The Catapult 'cast'

catapult 'cast' the line is short and is fairly easy to manage, even on a rod held low.

In Chapter Five I referred to a method of fishing deep water. Whilst I do not consider that fishing in such water is clear-water worm fishing in the proper sense, the same procedure may be applied to the deeper pools in a fast stream, which are quite properly worming water. You should put a tiny but freely working swivel on the cast about two feet from the bait and, having swung the latter up the pool, allow it to sink. Then lift the rod and work the bait downstream with a slow sink-and-draw movement. This action need only be very slight where there is a strong swirl of water in a deep hole, but a pronounced sink-and-draw motion is often effective in tempting a trout in the dead water on the fringes of the central current.

Another point already raised requires more detailed consideration. It concerns the use of shot generally. If you study the very scanty literature of clear-water bait fishing you will find that writers are fairly evenly divided in their opinions on this. For my part, I advise most strongly against shotting the cast; except for the catapult cast it is, in my view, quite unnecessary. There are, moreover, several very decided objections to its general use.

It is apt to cause the bait to be rolled along the bottom and to catch between stones. The shot rubs bright in time, or collects a wisp of algae and thus offsets all that you have gained by using fine nylon. If water is so rough that shot is necessary to keep it below the surface, then it is too rough for feeding trout to lie there. They are more likely to be on the edges of it, or in some small quieter area, and there your bait, carried by the current, will go down to them by its own weight and in *a natural manner*.

In moderately fast water and in true worming water generally, the bait should travel unhampered, in the grip of the current. In hard-bottomed streams – and most fast-running waters are that – bottom feed is not so plentiful as in slower waters. The trout feed largely upon food of various types carried down to them in suspension. Such food is the produce of a considerable area upstream from the trouts' positions and the latter are chosen by their tenants as being points where, owing to configuration of stream-bed or banks and their influence on the flow, such food is easily secured. You may be fairly certain that trout are capable of securing anything that drifts past within sight, or within normal feeding range. If this was not the case, the fish would not lie at those points. A worm floating naturally over or past trout can easily be taken by the fish if it wants it, and no shot is necessary to slow down its progress.

It is sometimes argued that, even if the undesirability of shotting is admitted, there is something to be said for it as a means of controlling the swinging line in windy weather. Well, I agree, of course, but there are other casts for windy weather, as I have tried to show, and I do not admit that the trifling advantage of shotting outweighs the handicap of a sluggish, jerkily dragging bait.

And lastly, if the use of shot had nothing else against it, the fact that it makes it impossible to keep the line always downstream from the bait would be sufficient to condemn it. You can see what happens if you drop a shotted and baited cast in a clear shallow run where you can watch it. One pellet of lead will be sufficient. Sooner or later, as the current eases, the shot sinks to the bottom and there catches on something; immediately the bait streams out on a short length of nylon, and above the hitched-up shot there is a belly that would in itself render detection of a bite impossible.

7

Bites and their Interpretation

THE study of the way of a trout with a worm is one of the most fascinating aspects of clear-water bait fishing, and you will find that the fullness of your knowledge on this point is gained, by experience, in three stages.

First of all, you learn to recognize the visible signs of a bite, second you learn – and in a school governed by stern disappointment – when to strike, and lastly you acquire the ability to analyse each stoppage of your bait, to decide whether the fish responsible is a good trout or a fingerling, and whether you will take the bait away or allow the bite to develop.

Of these the third is least important so far as its effect on your bag is concerned, and you will find that you can maintain a very decent average weight in the fish you kill if you remember that you must not allow the bait to rest idly, as it will on a very slack line. Thus you will avoid taking undersized fish. Until you have acquired the nicety of judgment which tells you what size of fish is (in all probability) tapping at the bait, scrupulous observance of the tight line rule will keep you out of trouble. Small trout and parr will, unfortunately, gorge a small worm, complete with hook tackle, in an amazingly short time, but few are badly hooked if, as I say, you keep the bait in fast water, with a straight line, or you know how to tell when one of these small nuisances takes the bait.

We have already discussed rod movement, which is designed to keep the line straight while the bait is drifting. What happens when a bite is seen or felt? Well, to begin with, the rod movement should not be arrested until the bait has, obviously, ceased to travel downstream. Then and then only should marked upward lift of the rod cease. The slight movement that should follow must be very delicately made and be just sufficient to take the last suspicion of slackness out of the line and to enable you to feel the bite.

Trout bites vary enormously according to the situation in which the taking fish is lying, the speed of the current and of the bait's drift, the size of the fish and the time of day.

The commonest bite is that indicated by a sudden stoppage of the travelling line, and since it enables you to strike with, and perhaps after, due deliberation, it is in some ways the easiest bite to deal with. Also common is the type of bite obtained when fishing isolated lies. You will often find that, when you are fishing a 'one-fish' lie located, say, just below an isolated boulder, as the bait comes down past the lie you will get a quick fierce pull, or perhaps two in rapid succession. These fish are usually good ones, and the best thing you can do is to give them just the least bit of slack for a few seconds before striking. What happens is that, unlike the fish that hovers in open water to meet a descending bait, our hidden friend sees the bait dance suddenly into view beside his lie and often has to pursue it downstream for a couple of feet before he grabs it. If he is given slack he begins to move back to his lie at once, swallowing his prize *en route*; if he feels a firm resistance he at once lets go (unless he has hooked himself in his rash grab), and he will not come again.

Then there is the quick, strong snatch at the bait which comes from a fish located beneath a bank washed by a strong current, and the dead solid stoppage that feels like a snag at first but, when it *is* a fish, is usually a heavy one. In both cases the fish often hook themselves by the very boldness of their taking.

A good fish sometimes takes a bait in somewhat slack water without giving any sign that it has done so. This can easily happen, because, whilst you must not allow the worm to lie, you cannot drag it, nor move it faster than it would be carried naturally by the current – unless you are fishing in very deep water by the sink-and-draw method. In fishing mixed water, some of which may be shallow, some deep, some very fast and some flowing just enough to keep the bait in motion, it is inevitable that the speed of the bait must be less than you would like it to be, at times. It is then that you may easily have a fish at the bait without your knowing it.

But bite variations are endless, and you will hardly meet two fish taking in precisely the same manner in a day's fishing in the average stream. One other and particularly 'difficult' type of offer occurs to me; fortunately it is not very common. It arises when a trout is stationed on the edge of fast water and takes its food therefrom by means of occasional forays into the stream. Such fish will sometimes take a bait in plain sight of the angler and it is rather a nerve-racking business to see a trout issue from his lair, seize the bait, and retreat with it. One's instinctive reaction is to strike at once, and though such a course is not always wise perhaps, in some cases the fish will be securely hooked simply because he is moving across or upstream when the strike is made. The hooks then usually take secure hold. What one must *not* do in any event is to take the bait away from him by lifting the rod as he appears, nor to strike before he has turned and is making away.

Small fish bite most boldly as a rule, I think, but not always, for good fish really feeding leave one in no doubt as to their intentions. At times, however, all trout are slow and cautious, and the best of them may bite with the faint nibblings of little fellows. You will find that when small trout and parr are most actively on the feed, the better fish are 'off' and vice versa. The little ones do not flaunt their attractions so freely when big fish are moving about and feeding. I have often wondered whether we are safe in attributing the comparative scarcity of small fish whilst big ones are moving to the reason I have suggested, or whether the difference in the times of greatest activity is due to age-habits in the two classes of fish. But there can be no doubt that biggish trout, quite apart from their cannibalistic tendencies, are confirmed bullies and patently intolerant of the presence of the smaller fry in their immediate neighbourhood.

Open water produces more small fish in the average stream and on most fishing days, and the best trout come to the net from isolated lies and the fringes of fast runs and deeply-pocketed water.

The timing of the strike is extremely important. More fish are lost by hasty striking than by giving time, but the latter course can be carried too far and makes for slovenly hooking. The happy medium, the perfectly-timed strike, is an operation guided so much by instinct that it is difficult to describe. It is obvious that just as bites vary, so must the strike vary in its timing.

Some fish take longer to negotiate the bait than others after they have taken hold of it – much depends upon the mood of the fish and its size – and it would be unwise to strike at the first vibrant touch of a gingerly biter, or, on the other hand, to delay when another and bolder fish has grabbed the bait and is going away with it well inside his mouth.

It is therefore quite impossible to make any rule as to timing the strike. Each bite calls for a kind of quick calculation – an estimate of the chances of hooking that fish from that moment onwards – and your strike is prompted by instinctive recognition of the right moment. The most that I can say in guidance to a beginner is that I think the most frequently successful strike is that made during the first pause in the series of tiny jars which are felt on the line after a fish has stopped the bait. Only one thing can teach striking that will be wise in the majority of cases, and that is experience. Even the best worm fisherman must miss a number of fish.

The action of striking is, in itself, quite simple. It consists of a trifling but sharp upward lift of the rod-tip – just that. The strike used in fly work is often described as a 'turn of the wrist', and I think that is merely an inadequate and quite misleading description of a wrist movement which lifts the rod top and straightens the line. No turning of the wrist is necessary either in fly or bait fishing, though the action of striking is precisely the same, except that in worm fishing the movement need not be the lightning response sometimes necessary to hook a fish rising to the fly. It can be more deliberate, partly because the fish is more or less stationary, and partly because there is not the same need to offset the softness of the rod-top. The worming rod, if properly designed, transmits the strike with very little preliminary dip.

I have used the word 'upward' in suggesting the action of striking, but I should perhaps substitute 'downstream' to suit some circumstances. The upward movement, made when the angler is well below his fish, hooks most surely, but it is sometimes necessary, in awkward or overgrown places, to hold the rod low and strike downstream as well as one can. Whatever the *angle* of the strike, it should never be anything but firm and controlled. If you find that the line, or rather the cast, whips from the water when you strike and miss a fish, then you are striking much too hard. Such force is quite unnecessary. Your line is, or should be, straight, and a movement of a few inches is sufficient to tighten it and drive home the small sharp hooks of the tackle.

The act of hooking a fish, then, may be dissected in this way. You see or feel a bite and at once the rod is raised very gently until the line is quite straight and you are in direct touch with the bait without pulling on it. Then, at what seems to be the proper instant, you strike by lifting the rod-top briskly – a movement which should not cease abruptly, be it noted, on your feeling the weight of the fish, but which should merge into the steady pressure designed to play it.

Now we come to the third degree (which sounds unpleasant but is not) of skill in handling bites – the ability to distinguish between the attentions of small fish and those of big ones, and by *this* means to avoid hooking small undesirables. At the outset it may be pointed out that even the most experienced are not infallible in this respect because, as I have said, there is such wide variation in the trout's ways of taking, and we can all make mistakes.

Parr swarm in their thousands in many seatrout and salmon rivers, and fall greedily upon any and every item of food that comes within their ken. Naturally they can be, and often are, an unmitigated nuisance to the worm-fisher; they mutilate the bait and waste his time, and *if given a chance* will gorge the tackle so badly that they cannot survive removal of the hooks. Their killing is both illegal and unsportsmanlike and is to be avoided at all costs.

You may ask, with reason, 'Why all this? You said at the beginning of this chapter that the killing of small fish could be avoided by never allowing the bait to rest.' Well, I did, and it is true, but the finished clear-water worm fisherman should not be content to rest upon that rule, though he will never do much good unless he bears it so clearly in mind that its observance becomes second nature.

It is not quite enough, however, and he gains additional insurance against the attentions of small fry by the ability to recognize their bites. Some of them will be found to take a bait in quite fast water, and if he relied absolutely upon the constant movement of the bait and upon that alone, to escape the parr, he would be certain to kill a few from time to time.

The complete solution of the problem lies not only in giving the small fish little opportunity to tackle the bait, but in being able to take it away from the odd ones that do, before they can take it properly. It is simple enough, with experience, to know the bite of a little fellow and to get the bait away.

Probably he will already have nipped the worm, of course, but re-baiting is a small matter. Nor is there any need for fear about disturbing the water where this kind of drop and lift away again business is frequent. Worm-fishing works water where trout are localized and the disturbance of one pocket matters little. In any case, the better fish are seldom among the little ones, and no harm is done when the worm suddenly soars away.

Anyone may learn easily enough how to recognize the usual form of parr bite, though trout of similar size are slower in biting and a little more difficult to detect. Take a light fly rod and put up some very small flies. Cast over some minnow-haunted shallow and let the fish nibble at the flies. The jerky tap-tap – tap tap on the line is precisely the 'feel' of a parr bite to the worm. You may know the small fish by that as a rule. The exceptions infuse a good deal of uncertainty into bite interpretation, and it is here that experience is so very valuable.

The man who can apply the general principles of the game, whilst bringing to his aid the finesse which is the product of painstaking observation, has a twofold advantage from the moment his bait halts in the stream. He wastes less time, uses fewer baits, and takes fish of a better average size than his fellows of less experience, and that, I think, is ample reward for study to be proficient.

I think I may end this chapter appropriately enough with a few suggestions on the handling of hooked fish. You should try always to play your fish so that it does not disturb water as yet unfished. With the average stream trout it is not difficult to keep him plunging and darting within a small area just ahead and hardly beyond the rod-tip. A fish over, say, three-quarters of a pound, cannot be held so hard on very fine nylon, and you must risk spoiling some water by letting him work at longer range if he wants. A bigger fish should be given line if he is determined to run, and he is safer, from your point of view, if he is well upstream from you and the current does not aid him in straining your tackle.

The usual run of takeable stream trout may be five to eight ounces in weight and these fish are easily held under the rod point and, when quiet, can be allowed to come downstream into the waiting net. How you handle the rod and net thereafter depends largely on your personal dexterity. I find it most convenient, when wading and using the long-handled net, to keep the rod in my right hand and use the net in my left. If I get hold of a fish that seems likely to take line and render use of the reel necessary, I pass the rod to my left hand (the net is secured to that wrist but hangs well out of the way) and shift it back when the fish is ready for netting. I do not find the changing over any trouble, since it is done almost unconsciously at the proper time.

Whether the fish is small or big, I use the net in my left hand and, when the fish is safely in the pouch, push the butt of the rod into my right wader, or, if there are trees overhead, tuck it up under my armpit. In either case it leaves my right hand free to take the fish – with a perfectly dry hand (if I propose to keep the fish) and a firm grip – from the net. I hold it rather close to the head and strike the latter hard on the net handle. I have only known two fish out of many hundreds killed in this way, to fly out of my grasp, and in spite of the slight risk of losing a fish, I much prefer it to that method which necessitates placing the thumb in the trout's mouth and bending the head back. This disfigures the fish and, in any case, can easily lacerate the thumb if the victim is of any size.

Handling the rod and net when you are fishing from the bank is a very simple matter by comparison, since the rod can be put down altogether and the fish removed from the net on terra firma. But whether you are wading or bank fishing, you should kill the fish, if it is of takeable size, before you remove the hooks. And here you will find the little bone disgorger wonderfully useful.

8

Approaching the Water – Wading – Concealment

IN SUGGESTING some of the probable 'lies' of trout, I dwelt on the need for a preliminary survey of the water to be fished. You will find that this is much simplified by the fact that most streams are naturally cut up into sections by lengths of impassable banks, reaches of deep water, or by other obstacles which prevent you from working steadily upstream. It is really all to the good, because it enables you to treat each section of stream separately and according to a plan suggested by its individual features. Tactics of this kind are infinitely preferable to tackling a long stretch of water of which you cannot pre-survey more than the lowest and nearest portion.

Much depends upon the character of the stream-bed and of the banks, of course, but the easiest kind of water to fish is that which is so featured that you are able to look over twenty or twenty-five yards of water before you begin to fish at the lower end of it. With more water than this ahead of you, you are apt to spoil too much of it. True, it opens up before you as you progress up-steam and you are always calculating the chances offered by the next few yards of water, but the point is that in this way you will often find yourself forced to approach the best water from what turns out to be the wrong angle. This would have been avoided had the area before you been small enough for close inspection.

You should try therefore to look at the whole of the section you are about to fish, before you begin. If you cannot do so from below, walk upstream – keeping as far back from the water as you can – and decide which are the important parts of it, and how you must work up to them. All of this slows down your fishing considerably but makes all the difference to your results.

So, having decided where your best chances of finding fish are, you have to approach them, and here you have to study background, the position of the sun, and the contour of the stream-bed.

Sometimes you cannot avoid wading, and at others all the useful water can be covered from the bank, but whichever position you adopt, you should always try to get down as near to water-level as possible. You are, naturally, lowest when wading and there is always the temptation to achieve a degree of concealment by entering the water. Unless you propose to wade only in the very shallow margin, close under the bank, it is a great mistake to enter the water in streams of a size that may be covered from the bank. However cautious you may be, wading disturbs far too many trout. You do not kick them up as you do hares in a rough pasture – you disturb them at long range, particularly in unbroken water, and though you cannot know it you are probably frightening trout for yards around you. In big rivers, of course, wading is essential if you are to work the water thoroughly.

Personally, I always *wear* waders even when fishing small streams, partly for convenience in crossing to and fro, and partly because, where the skyline is low, the best approach to much of the water is down at the foot of the banks, at the shallow edge of each pool. Creeping forward there, in an inch or two of water, you are as low as you would be if you took properly to the water, but you disturb it a great deal less.

I do not hesitate to kneel in the shallows if need be, though it is not a practice particularly kind to waders. But if you would stalk trout you must creep and crawl and sit on your heels and do everything except show yourself. I think I must have crawled along many miles of hill-stream margins, with the dippers and the curlews for company, in the course of each season, and enjoyed every moment of it. Indeed, the taking of a half-pound trout from some crystal pool after a difficult stalk is quite an event. You have planned your approach, worked for your fish and got him, and that is, or ought to be, of the stuff that is the real joy in angling.

On small streams, then, you should stay on the bank or near to it, keep below the skyline and take advantage of rocks and bushes and all the cover you can find. Watch your background all the time and try to visualize how you fit into it – not from your own eye level, but from that of the trout down in the stream. The fish to which you are offering your bait cannot see you unless you happen, at the moment, to be fishing up and across, or across, but those more nearly opposite to you and probably already fished over, can see you. They will dash upstream, if alarmed, and there frighten others over which you have not yet had a chance to fish.

As a rule it is best to fish each pool or run from the shallow side and, whether you wade or not, you should try to avoid having the sun behind you. Or, if you like, you can put it this way – avoid fishing in such a light that you can see the bottom with unusual clarity a few steps ahead. If you bear this in mind you cannot go far wrong. In all your movements be quiet and unhurried – that too is important.

Special care is always necessary in approaching that portion of a pool which carries an eddy or back-wash; you may be quite hidden from trout lying in the ordinary position with heads upstream and perfectly visible to fish hovering facing the stream in the eddy.

In the larger streams and in big rivers you will have to wade and, if the depth and strength of the current will allow you, you cannot do better than wade in midstream. From this position you can cover a great deal of water, fishing ahead and on both sides. The straight upstream cast, which can hardly arise in bank fishing, is not a very good one, because the fish see the gut before they see the bait. Those casts made up and *slightly* across present the bait from the best possible angle.

If a stream is big enough to justify midstream wading your solid background will be rather distant for you to take much advantage of it. Out in a big river you are silhouetted against the sky in all probability, and the most you can do is to move deliberately, avoid handling bright tackle boxes or anything that flashes in the sun, and wade slowly.

Good wading is quite an art, and for the man fishing frequently in wide rivers, well worth studying. There are two things to be watched – one, that you take ordinary precautions for your own safety and, two, that you do not spoil the water by clumsy wading.

Do not, if you can avoid it, wade a strange river without first making enquiries as to any danger spots that there may be, and, in the absence of such advice – do not wade without the help of your wading-staff landing net. Grope your way forward with this. Always test the bottom and the depth in two or three places with the staff before you step forward. These are elementary precautions, but very wise ones. Some rivers abound in pot-holes and a false step, though it may not precipitate you directly into dangerous water, may cause a fall which, in fast, heavy water, will be serious.

I have had one such experience and found it the reverse of amusing, and I have also narrowly escaped disaster while fishing a different type of water. I was wading close to the bank, in a North of England river, on a firm pebble and clay matrix over which flowed a strong current about nine inches deep. The body of the pool, some way out and above me, was very deep, I knew. I pushed my staff forward and probed ahead even as I moved my foot forward, and to my astonishment could find no bottom! The ledge – it was no more than that – simply petered out unseen beneath the bubbling water. Later I found a warning to anglers nailed to a nearby elm, and later still I was told that there was eighteen feet of water beyond and under the overhanging ledge.

So much for safety, and now let us look at good and bad wading from the point of view of their effects on sport.

You should always enter the water well down-stream from the point where your first throw is to be made. Work out to your position by taking a diagonal course across and up. This is much easier than wading across the current and then working up. The water does not push so hard against you and you make less disturbance. Cross-stream wading is very bad, for you are unsteady owing to the push in your legs and therefore clumsy.

Once in your fishing position, you should make no more major moves until you have fished that area out. Then move slowly without lifting your brogues to the surface. Try to test each foothold before placing your weight on it, lifting your feet just enough to clear obstructions and no more. Avoid kicking against stones as much as possible, and never wade in the smooth glassy tails of streams. The surges you would make by so doing might not travel far upstream, but they would alarm successive batches of fish until the water was spoiled, perhaps right up to the head of the pool.

Always regard gravel patches with distrust; they slip and grind beneath your feet and betray your presence more than you may think.

When you have apparently exhausted the possibilities in one stretch of water and find, as you often will, that you have to wade ashore to go farther upstream, do so cautiously. It may happen that there remain one of two promising bits of water between you and the bank, or just above the point where you intend to leave the water. It is annoying to discover that careless wading has deprived you of several promising casts which you had not seen from mid-stream.

For summer wading I think lightweight fabric waders, if you can get them, socks and brogues are, when everything is taken into consideration, less tiring than rubber boots. The latter even the new thin variety are inclined to be hot, in my experience, and more inclined to chafe one's heels on days when much clambering up steep banks has to be done. Rubbers are handy, of course, and easily slipped on and off, and this is their best recommendation. I do not think they are cheaper than the best fabric waders and good brogues of canvas and leather, in the long run. They are difficult to dry properly and any lining soon rots. The uppers are not markedly longer-lived when you are kneeling in them frequently than those of fabric. The latter can be reinforced at the knee quite simply by adding an exterior patch with rubber solution.

In any case, whichever outfit you favour, see that the soles and heels *and the instep* are well studded, or are of felt. Moss and algae is most abundant in late summer when water is low and in these conditions a stony bottom can be extremely slippery.

Lastly, there is the question of clothes. So that you may not mar all of your endeavours to be inconspicuous, wear the oldest, most weather-stained fishing clothes that you have. Don't, on any account, exhibit any expanse of white collar and shirt – the splash of white simply won't fit into any of nature's backgrounds except perhaps the sky. But this is the worst background you can have, and you should always aim at concealment among the masses and colour tones of a solid background.

*   *   *   *

It seems that there are many 'musts' and 'do's' and 'don'ts' scattered through the preceding pages, and a mass of detail which may be a little bewildering to a beginner. The fault, if fault it is, rests with my anxiety to give as full and complete a description of every aspect of clear-water worm fishing as is possible. I hope that the unavoidable repetition of some points has not strained the patience of my readers and that the beginner will not find anything of discouragement in the detail he is asked to study.

Index